MW01076250

Ancient Book of
Daniel

By Ken Johnson, Th.D.

Copyright 2010, by Ken Johnson, Th.D.

Ancient Book of Daniel
by Ken Johnson, Th.D.

Printed in the United States of America

ISBN   1456306561
EAN-13   9781456306564

Drawings from Clearance Larkin's book, *Dispensational Truth*, 1907

Unless otherwise indicated, Bible quotations are taken from the King James Version.

Contents

Introduction 5

Daniel 1 9

Daniel 2 15

Daniel 3 27

Daniel 4 35

Daniel 5 43

Daniel 6 59

Daniel 7 65

Daniel 8 75

Daniel 9 85

Daniel 10 103

Daniel 11 109

Daniel 12 129

Timeline Prophecies 135

The Fall Festivals 141

Appendix A Ancient Church Commentary 151

Appendix B Tribulation Outline 163

Other Books by Ken Johnson, Th.D. 167

Bibliography 172

Dedicated in memory of my father,
Kenneth W. Johnson, Sr.
1916-2010

Introduction

The ancient book of Daniel records the prophecies God gave to the prophet Daniel warning the Jews to repent of their sins and predicting numerous future events. Among these are prophecies that Messiah would die in AD 32 and that the nation of Israel would be reestablished in AD 1948. Daniel also predicted which country the Antichrist will come from and where he will create his international headquarters. He predicted a pre-tribulational Rapture of believers and many other things set to occur during our lifetimes.

Divine Inspiration
Today there are several commentaries that teach Daniel was written in the first century BC by someone who wanted to encourage the Jews to fight against the Romans by making up prophecies about the past. These liberal commentaries suggest that Daniel chapter 11 is too accurate in its prophecies to be written beforehand. In other words, they do not believe in the reality of prophecies and suggest, in a very polite way, the book of Daniel is all lies. We will show you that Daniel not only predicted many events in the distant past and our future, but he also accurately predicted the return of the nation of Israel to occur in May 1948 and that Israel would retake the Temple Mount in June of 1967. These and other prophecies prove beyond a shadow of a doubt that Daniel is a real prophet and every single prediction given in his

book is indeed real! Our Lord Jesus even said we are foolish if we do not believe all of the prophecies!

> "Then he said unto them, O fools, and slow of heart
> to believe all that the prophets have spoken:"
> *Luke 24:25*

Premillennialism

Many of Daniel's prophecies center on the Messianic kingdom. Both the ancient church and most Bible-centered churches today teach what is called premillennialism. Premillennialism simply means the reign of Jesus Christ will be a literal one thousand years and will begin in the future after the Tribulation. Events predicted to occur around the seven-year Tribulation, the Antichrist, and the Second Coming will take place in the near future. Other churches teach amillennialism. Amillennialism teaches that these events are symbolic of something else and occurred centuries ago, effectively canceling out real prophecy.

In Appendix A we will reveal numerous quotes from the first and second century church fathers, which will show the reader that both the ancient church and the apostles were premillennialists. Therefore, when Daniel predicted something to occur in the "latter days" or the "end time" he was referring to the seven-year Tribulation, and when he wrote about the eleventh horn, little horn, or willful king, he was referring to the future Antichrist. We get the name Antichrist from 1 John, but it applies to the same person. See Appendix A for complete details.

Outline

It is important to understand when Daniel received his visions and when each recorded event took place. Look at the following chart.

Reference	Description	Date
Daniel 1	Third year of Jehoiakim	607 BC
Daniel 2	Second Year of Nebuchadnezzar	605 BC
Daniel 3	Sometime after chapter 2	? BC
Daniel 4	Towards the end of Nebuchadnezzar's life	? BC
Daniel 7	First year of Belshazzar	539 BC
Daniel 8	Third year of Belshazzar	536 BC
Daniel 5	Death of Belshazzar	536 BC
Daniel 9	First year of Darius the Mede	536 BC
Daniel 10-12	Third year of Cyrus	533 BC
Daniel 6	Sometime after chapter 9	? BC

Daniel received the visions recorded in chapters 7 and 8 *before* chapter 5. Knowing this, one can see how Daniel immediately understood the handwriting on the wall.

The story of Daniel begins in the distant past. The nation of Israel truly began as a nation under Kings Saul and David. Solomon built the temple. At Solomon's death, the nation split into two: the northern kingdom kept the name Israel, and the southern kingdom was renamed Judah. In time, both nations turned away from the Lord. The Lord sent prophets to correct Israel and Judah but they refused to listen. God allowed Assyria to conquer the northern nation of Israel in 722 BC. Later, in 612 BC, the Babylonians conquered the Assyrians, destroying their capital city of Nineveh.

Even though the Assyrian dispersion of Israel took place exactly as the prophet Nahum predicted, Judah still would not repent; so God allowed the Babylonians to conquer Judah. The prophet Isaiah predicted this about 800 BC, almost two hundred years before the prophecy was fulfilled.

> "Then said Isaiah to Hezekiah, Hear the word of the LORD of hosts: Behold, the days come, that all that *is* in thine house, and *that* which thy fathers have laid up in store until this day, shall be carried to Babylon: nothing shall be left, saith the LORD. And of thy sons that shall issue from thee, which thou shalt beget, shall they take away; and they shall be eunuchs in the palace of the king of Babylon.
> *Isaiah 39:5-7*

In 607 BC, Babylonian King Nebuchadnezzar attacked Jerusalem and took the first wave of captives back to Babylon. Daniel was among these captives. In 597 BC King Nebuchadnezzar crushed the beginnings of a rebellion and took a second wave of captives. In 587 BC he destroyed Solomon's temple and the city of Jerusalem.

Daniel began his book by focusing on Isaiah's prophecy about Babylon.

Thus begins the story of Daniel...

Daniel
1

Isaiah 39:5-7 Fulfilled

Daniel records the fulfillment of Isaiah's prediction that the temple vessels would be taken to Babylon.

"[1]In the third year of the reign of Jehoiakim king of Judah came Nebuchadnezzar king of Babylon unto Jerusalem, and besieged it. [2]And the Lord gave Jehoiakim king of Judah into his hand, with part of the vessels of the house of God: which he carried into the land of Shinar to the house of his god; and he brought the vessels into the treasure house of his god." *Daniel 1:1-2*

According to the twenty-fifth chapter of the Jewish history book, *Ancient Seder Olam*, the third year of Jehoiakim's reign would have been about 607 BC. Both Josephus and Daniel testify to the second part of Isaiah's prediction that Daniel, Hananiah, Mishael, and Azariah were the Jews from the royal court that were predicted to be taken captive and made into eunuchs.

"Nebuchadnezzar, king of Babylon, took some of the most noble of the Jews that were children, and the kinsmen of Zedekiah their king... and delivered them into the hands of tutors, and to the improvement to be made by them. He also made some of them to be eunuchs... and had them instructed in the institutes of the country, and taught the learning of the Chaldeans; and they had now exercised themselves sufficiently in that wisdom which he had ordered they should apply themselves to. Now among these there were four of the family of Zedekiah, of most excellent dispositions, one of whom was called Daniel; another was called Ananias, another Misael, and the fourth Azarias." *Josephus Antiquities 10.10.1*

"[3]And the king spake unto Ashpenaz the master of his eunuchs, that he should bring *certain* of the children of Israel, and of the king's seed, and of the princes; [4]Children in whom *was* no blemish, but well favoured, and skilful in all wisdom, and cunning in knowledge, and understanding science, and such as *had* ability in them to stand in the king's palace, and whom they might teach the learning and the tongue of the Chaldeans. [5]And the king appointed them a daily provision of the king's meat, and of the wine which he drank: so nourishing them three years, that at the end thereof they might stand before the king." *Daniel 1:3-5*

It was customary to take the brightest from a captive nation and teach them the native Babylonian language. Three years also gave enough time to prove they were not carrying any disease.

Daniel and Friends' Names Changed

Daniel, whose Hebrew name means "God is Judge," was given the Babylonian name of Belteshazzar, which means "prince of Bel." Hananiah, whose Hebrew name means "Yahweh is gracious," was renamed the Babylonian Shadrach, which means "command of Aku." Aku was an Akkadian moon god. Mishael, whose Hebrew name means "who is like God?" was given the Babylonian name of Meshach, which means "who is what Aku is?" Azariah, whose Hebrew name means "Yahweh has helped," was renamed the Babylonian Abednego, which means "servant of Nebo." Nebo was the Babylonian god of wisdom.

> "⁶Now among these were of the children of Judah, Daniel, Hananiah, Mishael, and Azariah: ⁷Unto whom the prince of the eunuchs gave names: for he gave unto Daniel *the name* of Belteshazzar; and to Hananiah, of Shadrach; and to Mishael, of Meshach; and to Azariah, of Abednego."
> *Daniel 1:6-7*

It is interesting to note that if you string together the Hebrew names of Mishael, Hananiah, and Azariah, you form a sentence which can read "the one who is like God [Jesus the Messiah] will bring Yahweh's grace and help." If you string together the Babylonian names they mean absolutely nothing. To me this reveals God is in complete control even to the point of giving you your name! I have often wondered why you always hear the names Daniel, Shadrach, Meshach, and Abednego instead of Daniel,

Hananiah, Mishael, and Azariah. Maybe Satan is trying to keep us from focusing on God's sovereignty!

Following God, Not Man

Daniel and his friends were not vegetarians. They were forbidden to eat *certain* meat like pork. This law was never binding on Christians; it was for the Jews back in that time. The apostle Paul states in 1 Timothy 4:1-3, that the idea that vegetarianism would help you get closer to God is a doctrine of demons that will manifest in the last days. It was dangerous for the young men to obey God and not eat many of the common foods of Babylon. Refusing to obey the king could lead to imprisonment or death. But Daniel and his friends took that chance because they loved God more than their own lives.

If Daniel risked his life for his testimony, will you risk getting fired? Will you even risk being laughed at at work or by your friends? We are persecuted so little in the USA and yet still cannot seem to stand up for our faith in the smallest ways!

> "[8]But Daniel purposed in his heart that he would not defile himself with the portion of the king's meat, nor with the wine which he drank: therefore he requested of the prince of the eunuchs that he might not defile himself. [9]Now God had brought Daniel into favour and tender love with the prince of the eunuchs. [10]And the prince of the eunuchs said unto Daniel, I fear my lord the king, who hath appointed your meat and your drink: for why should he see

your faces worse liking than the children which *are* of your sort? then shall ye make *me* endanger my head to the king. [11]Then said Daniel to Melzar, whom the prince of the eunuchs had set over Daniel, Hananiah, Mishael, and Azariah, [12]Prove thy servants, I beseech thee, ten days; and let them give us pulse to eat, and water to drink. [13]Then let our countenances be looked upon before thee, and the countenance of the children that eat of the portion of the king's meat: and as thou seest, deal with thy servants. [14]So he consented to them in this matter, and proved them ten days. [15]And at the end of ten days their countenances appeared fairer and fatter in flesh than all the children which did eat the portion of the king's meat. [16]Thus Melzar took away the portion of their meat, and the wine that they should drink; and gave them pulse.
Daniel 1:8-16

Notice Daniel was not hateful or demanding with his master (boss), but respectfully tried to work out a compromise. We should always show respect to those in authority. This is the way God would have us live our lives. God is in control; and if we dedicate our lives to Him, He will protect us.

"[17]As for these four children, God gave them knowledge and skill in all learning and wisdom: and Daniel had understanding in all visions and dreams. [18]Now at the end of the days that the king had said he should bring them in, then the prince of the

eunuchs brought them in before Nebuchadnezzar. [19]And the king communed with them; and among them all was found none like Daniel, Hananiah, Mishael, and Azariah: therefore stood they before the king. [20]And in all matters of wisdom *and* understanding, that the king enquired of them, he found them ten times better than all the magicians and astrologers[a] that were in all his realm."
Daniel 1:17-20

Daniel studied science and the Scriptures making him wiser that anyone else who only studied one or the other. We should do the same. Daniel was an expert in dreams and visions. We, too, could become experts in dreams and visions *if* we study the prophecies seriously and literally. I encourage you to study the book of Daniel well, to learn not only of God's faithfulness in the past, but of your future as well!

"[21]And Daniel continued *even* unto the first year of king Cyrus." *Daniel 1:21*

Daniel started ruling in 604 BC under King Nebuchadnezzar and continued beyond the year Cyrus the Persian conquered Babylon, 536 BC. His career spanned more than seventy years.

---

[a] For a complete discussion of magicians and astrologers see the book *Ancient Paganism.*

Daniel
2

Nebuchadnezzar's Forgotten Dream

Halfway through Daniel's three-year trial period, in the second year of Nebuchadnezzar's rule, the king had a dream he thought was extremely important. This would have occurred about 605 BC. He did not want pagans making up an interpretation; so he refused to describe the dream. If someone could tell him the dream, then he would know the interpretation from that same person would be accurate.

"¹And in the second year of the reign of Nebuchadnezzar, Nebuchadnezzar dreamed dreams, wherewith his spirit was troubled, and his sleep brake from him. ²Then the king commanded to call the magicians, and the astrologers, and the sorcerers, and the Chaldeans, for to shew the king his dreams. So they came and stood before the king. ³And the king said unto them, I have dreamed a dream, and my spirit was troubled to know the dream. ⁴Then spake the Chaldeans to the king in Syriac, O king, live for ever: tell thy servants the dream, and we will shew the interpretation. ⁵The king answered and said to the Chaldeans, The thing is gone from me: if ye will not make known unto me the dream, with the interpretation thereof, ye shall be cut in pieces, and your houses shall be made a dunghill. [6]But if ye shew the dream, and the interpretation thereof, ye shall receive of me gifts and rewards and great honour: therefore shew me the dream, and the interpretation thereof. [7]They answered again and said, Let the king tell his servants the dream, and we will shew the interpretation of it. [8]The king answered and said, I know of certainty that ye would gain the time, because ye see the thing is gone from me. [9]But if ye will not make known unto me the dream, *there is but* one decree for you: for ye have prepared lying and corrupt words to speak before me, till the time be changed: therefore tell me the dream, and I shall know that ye can shew me the interpretation thereof." *Daniel 2:1-9*

Test Prophets and Prove Them True or False

When a person claims to speak a word from God especially for you, there is nothing wrong with testing them. Ask them to tell you something they could not know, to see if they really do speak for God! God will hold each of us personally responsible for following a false prophet, instead of testing them. If you blindly follow a false prophet, you will receive the same punishment that he does.

"And they shall bear their punishment—the punishment of the inquirer and the punishment of the prophet shall be the same." *Ezekiel 14:10 NRSV*

The pagans told King Nebuchadnezzar it was impossible for them to tell him the dream. So, if Daniel accomplished this task, obviously his God was the one true God.

> "¹⁰The Chaldeans answered before the king, and said, There is not a man upon the earth that can shew the king's matter: therefore *there is* no king, lord, nor ruler, *that* asked such things at any magician, or astrologer, or Chaldean. ¹¹And *it is* a rare thing that the king requireth, and there is none other that can shew it before the king, except the gods, whose dwelling is not with flesh."
> *Daniel 2:10-11*

Nebuchadnezzar decided the pagans were useless; so he made a decree that all the wise men should be killed. This included Daniel. Daniel used this situation to witness to the king. He explained there was no way for him to know the dream, since he was just a man; but if the king allowed him to pray to his God and sleep overnight, God could give Daniel complete understanding of the dream. Then Daniel could properly interpret the dream for the king. Nebuchadnezzar agreed.

> "¹²For this cause the king was angry and very furious, and commanded to destroy all the wise *men* of Babylon. ¹³And the decree went forth that the wise *men* should be slain; and they sought Daniel and his fellows to be slain. ¹⁴Then Daniel answered with counsel and wisdom to Arioch the captain of the king's guard, which was gone forth to slay the

wise *men* of Babylon: [15]He answered and said to Arioch the king's captain, Why *is* the decree *so* hasty from the king? Then Arioch made the thing known to Daniel. [16]Then Daniel went in, and desired of the king that he would give him time, and that he would shew the king the interpretation." *Daniel 2:12-16*

The Secret is Revealed to Daniel

Daniel asked Hananiah, Mishael, and Azariah to pray with him. The New Testament instructs us, as well, to call for the elders of the church to pray with us in times of trouble. God showed his mercy to the Jews and his sovereignty and power to Nebuchadnezzar by allowing Daniel to have a vision of Nebuchadnezzar's secret dream.

"[17]Then Daniel went to his house, and made the thing known to Hananiah, Mishael, and Azariah, his companions: [18]That they would desire mercies of the God of heaven concerning this secret; that Daniel and his fellows should not perish with the rest of the wise *men* of Babylon. [19]Then was the secret revealed unto Daniel in a night vision. Then Daniel blessed the God of heaven." *Daniel 2:17-19*

Daniel Praises God

Daniel praised God by recognizing His sovereignty, omnipotence, and omniscience.

"[20]Daniel answered and said, Blessed be the name of God for *ever* and ever: for wisdom and might are his: [21]And he changeth the times and the seasons: he removeth kings, and setteth up kings: he giveth wisdom unto the wise, and knowledge to them that know understanding: [22]He revealeth the deep and secret things: he knoweth what *is* in the darkness, and the light dwelleth with him. [23]I thank thee, and praise thee, O thou God of my fathers, who hast given me wisdom and might, and hast made known unto me now what we desired of thee: for thou hast *now* made known unto us the king's matter." *Daniel 2:20-23*

Daniel's Audience with the King

When Daniel stood before the King, he neither bragged nor belittled the pagans, but simply used this time to witness. If the pagans could not do the miracle that Daniel did, then maybe the king should change religions and worship the one true God. In all cases we should be as humble as Daniel was. Remember you are just being used by God. You are not doing anything by your own power.

"[24]Therefore Daniel went in unto Arioch, whom the king had ordained to destroy the wise *men* of Babylon: he went and said thus unto him; Destroy not the wise *men* of Babylon: bring me in before the king, and I will shew unto the king the interpretation. [25]Then Arioch brought in Daniel before the king in haste, and said thus unto him, I have found a man of the captives of Judah, that

will make known unto the king the interpretation. [26]The king answered and said to Daniel, whose name *was* Belteshazzar, Art thou able to make known unto me the dream which I have seen, and the interpretation thereof? [27]Daniel answered in the presence of the king, and said, The secret which the king hath demanded cannot the wise *men*, the astrologers, the magicians, the soothsayers[b], shew unto the king; [28]But there is a God in heaven that revealeth secrets, and maketh known to the king Nebuchadnezzar what shall be in the latter days. Thy dream, and the visions of thy head upon thy bed, are these; [29]As for thee, O king, thy thoughts came *into thy mind* upon thy bed, what should come to pass hereafter: and he that revealeth secrets maketh known to thee what shall come to pass. [30]But as for me, this secret is not revealed to me for *any* wisdom that I have more than any living, but for *their* sakes that shall make known the interpretation to the king, and that thou mightest know the thoughts of thy heart."
Daniel 2:24-30

The Dream of the Great Image

Daniel described the great image made of gold, silver, brass, iron, and clay and how the image was destroyed by a great rock.

---

[b] For a complete discussion of astrologers, magicians, and soothsayers, see the book *Ancient Paganism* by the author.

"[31]Thou, O king, sawest, and behold a great image. This great image, whose brightness *was* excellent, stood before thee; and the form thereof *was* terrible. [32]This image's head *was* of fine gold, his breast and his arms of silver, his belly and his thighs of brass, [33]His legs of iron, his feet part of iron and part of clay. [34]Thou sawest till that a stone was cut out without hands, which smote the image upon his feet *that were* of iron and clay, and brake them to pieces. [35]Then was the iron, the clay, the brass, the silver, and the gold, broken to pieces together, and became like the chaff of the summer threshingfloors; and the wind carried them away, that no place was found for them: and the stone that smote the image became a great mountain, and filled the whole earth. [36]This is the dream; and we will tell the interpretation thereof before the king."
Daniel 2:31-36

The Interpretation of the Image
The image Nebuchadnezzar saw in his dream represented four great kingdoms: Babylon, Medio-Persia, Greece, and Rome.

"[37]Thou, O king, *art* a king of kings: for the God of heaven hath given thee a kingdom, power, and strength, and glory. [38]And wheresoever the children of men dwell, the beasts of the field and the fowls of the heaven hath he given into thine hand, and hath made thee ruler over them all. Thou *art* this head of gold. [39]And after thee shall arise

> another kingdom inferior to thee, and another third kingdom of brass, which shall bear rule over all the earth. [40]And the fourth kingdom shall be strong as iron: forasmuch as iron breaketh in pieces and subdueth all *things*: and as iron that breaketh all these, shall it break in pieces and bruise."
> *Daniel 2:37-40*

In verse 38, Daniel told Nebuchadnezzar that the golden head represented his Babylonian Empire. Nebuchadnezzar became king and besieged Jerusalem in 607 BC. The Babylonian kingdom fell in 536 BC to the Medes and Persians. The fall is recorded in Daniel 5:30-31. Daniel 8:20-21 records the third kingdom would be Greece. The Persians ruled the Middle East until the Greeks, under Alexander the Great, conquered them in 323 BC. Greece fell to the Roman Empire, called Chittim (Rome's Hebrew name in Daniel 11:30). The Romans captured Jerusalem in 64 BC.

From top to bottom, the metals of the image changed from more valuable to less valuable. Shifting from gold to silver to brass then iron, is moving from a more precious, but weaker metal, to an ever more common and stronger metal. The Persians ruled more area than Babylon; likewise, Greece ruled even more territory. Rome commanded the largest territory of them all.

Division and Fall of the Roman Empire
The iron legs represented Rome at its strongest period. The feet composed of part iron and part clay represented

the time it was divided, and therefore weak. Rome remained strong and sovereign until it split into two separate kingdoms in AD 325. The eastern division ruled from Constantinople and the western division ruled from Rome. This division continued until AD 476 when both halves of Rome fell to invaders from the north. Having multiple leaders makes a kingdom weak.

> "^{41}And whereas thou sawest the feet and toes, part of potters' clay, and part of iron, the kingdom shall be divided; but there shall be in it of the strength of the iron, forasmuch as thou sawest the iron mixed with miry clay." *Daniel 2:41*

The Ten Toes

The feet and toes of the image are an outgrowth of the fallen iron Roman Empire. They will form some kind of democracy or confederacy; but will disagree on so many points that their government will be weak and ineffective. Since Rome fell in AD 476, and the kingdom of ten nations never formed, we know this part of the prophecy is yet future.

> "^{42}And *as* the toes of the feet *were* part of iron, and part of clay, *so* the kingdom shall be partly strong, and partly broken. ^{43}And whereas thou sawest iron mixed with miry clay, they shall mingle themselves with the seed of men: but they shall not cleave one to another, even as iron is not mixed with clay." *Daniel 2:42-43*

The Ancient Church

The Ancient church taught premillennialism. Church father Irenaeus, in AD 177, taught the Roman Empire would first be divided, then dissolved, based on Daniel 2:41. The division did not happen until AD 325, a hundred and forty-eight years later. The complete fall of the Roman Empire occurred two hundred and ninety-nine years after he wrote his commentary. Irenaeus also taught the ten toes are a revived Roman Empire that will exist prior to the Second Coming of Jesus Christ.[c]

The Millennium

While the revived Roman Empire still stands, the Messiah will return to earth and set up His Messianic kingdom. This also shows us that the ten-kingdom confederacy does not yet exist.

> "[44]And in the days of these kings shall the God of heaven set up a kingdom, which shall never be destroyed: and the kingdom shall not be left to other people, *but* it shall break in pieces and consume all these kingdoms, and it shall stand for ever. [45]Forasmuch as thou sawest that the stone was cut out of the mountain without hands, and that it brake in pieces the iron, the brass, the clay, the silver, and the gold; the great God hath made known to the king what shall come to pass hereafter: and the dream *is* certain, and the interpretation thereof sure." *Daniel 2:44-45*

---

[c] See Appendix A for the ancient church's view on these prophecies.

Daniel's Promotion

The Lord will reward a Christian truly dedicated to God and willing to be truthful in every situation.

"⁴⁶Then the king Nebuchadnezzar fell upon his face, and worshipped Daniel, and commanded that they should offer an oblation and sweet odours unto him. ⁴⁷The king answered unto Daniel, and said, Of a truth *it is*, that your God *is* a God of gods, and a Lord of kings, and a revealer of secrets, seeing thou couldest reveal this secret. ⁴⁸Then the king made Daniel a great man, and gave him many great gifts, and made him ruler over the whole province of Babylon, and chief of the governors over all the wise *men* of Babylon. ⁴⁹Then Daniel requested of the king, and he set Shadrach, Meshach, and Abednego, over the affairs of the province of Babylon: but Daniel *sat* in the gate of the king." *Daniel 2:46-49*

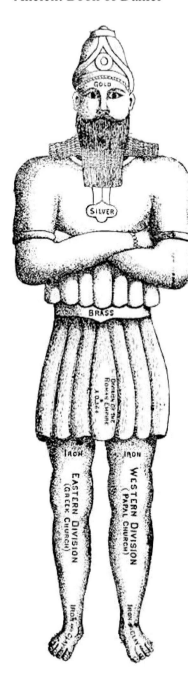

Babylon
607-536 BC
Daniel 2:38

Medeo-Persia
536-323 BC
Daniel 5:30-31

Greece
323-64 BC
Daniel 8:20-21

Rome
64 BC – AD 395
Daniel 11:30

Roman Division
AD 395-476
Daniel 2:41

Revived Roman Empire
End time
Seven-year Tribulation

Daniel

3

In time, Nebuchadnezzar forgot about Daniel's God and fell back into his old pagan ways. He created a large golden image based on the one in his dream. This was his way of saying that through magic and sorcery he could change the outcome of the prediction and create an empire that would last forever. He was wrong.

"¹Nebuchadnezzar the king made an image of gold, whose height *was* threescore cubits, *and* the breadth thereof six cubits: he set it up in the plain of Dura, in the province of Babylon. ²Then Nebuchadnezzar the king sent to gather together the princes, the governors, and the captains, the judges, the treasurers, the counsellors, the sheriffs, and all the rulers of the provinces, to come to the dedication of the image which Nebuchadnezzar the king had set up. ³Then the princes, the governors, and captains, the judges, the treasurers, the counsellors, the sheriffs, and all the rulers of the provinces, were gathered together unto the dedication of the image that Nebuchadnezzar the king had set up; and they stood before the image that Nebuchadnezzar had set up. ⁴Then an herald cried aloud, To you it is commanded, O people, nations, and languages, ⁵*That* at what time ye hear the sound of the cornet, flute, harp, sackbut, psaltery, dulcimer, and all kinds of musick, ye fall down and worship the golden image that Nebuchadnezzar the king hath set up: [6]And whoso falleth not down and worshippeth shall the same hour be cast into the midst of a burning fiery furnace." *Daniel 3:1-6*

666

Notice the size of the image was sixty cubits high and six cubits wide and that when six different kinds of musical instruments played, everyone had to worship the image or be put to death. This is a type, or picture, of the future image of the beast described in Revelation. It, too, is connected with the number 666;[d] and those who will not bow down and worship it will be killed.

Shadrach, Meshach, and Abednego Refuse to Bow

Obedient Christians and Jews never bow to idols, even if their lives depend upon it.

"[7]Therefore at that time, when all the people heard the sound of the cornet, flute, harp, sackbut, psaltery, and all kinds of musick, all the people, the nations, and the languages, fell down *and* worshipped the golden image that Nebuchadnezzar the king had set up. [8]Wherefore at that time certain Chaldeans came near, and accused the Jews. [9]They spake and said to the king Nebuchadnezzar, O king, live for ever. [10]Thou, O king, hast made a decree, that every man that shall hear the sound of the

---

[d] See Appendix A for the ancient church's view of the 666 prophecy.

cornet, flute, harp, sackbut, psaltery, and dulcimer, and all kinds of musick, shall fall down and worship the golden image: [11]And whoso falleth not down and worshippeth, *that* he should be cast into the midst of a burning fiery furnace. [12]There are certain Jews whom thou hast set over the affairs of the province of Babylon, Shadrach, Meshach, and Abednego; these men, O king, have not regarded thee: they serve not thy gods, nor worship the golden image which thou hast set up. [13]Then Nebuchadnezzar in *his* rage and fury commanded to bring Shadrach, Meshach, and Abednego. Then they brought these men before the king."
Daniel 3:7-13

Nebuchadnezzar's Question

Nebuchadnezzar threatened Shadrach, Meshach, and Abednego with death if they continued to refuse to worship the image.

"[14]Nebuchadnezzar spake and said unto them, *Is it* true, O Shadrach, Meshach, and Abednego, do not ye serve my gods, nor worship the golden image which I have set up? [15]Now if ye be ready that at what time ye hear the sound of the cornet, flute, harp, sackbut, psaltery, and dulcimer, and all kinds of musick, ye fall down and worship the image which I have made; *well*: but if ye worship not, ye shall be cast the same hour into the midst of a burning fiery furnace; and who *is* that God that shall deliver you out of my hands?" *Daniel 3:14-15*

The Reply

Shadrach, Meshach, and Abednego resolved never to bow to the idol. Whether God saved them or not, they would not disobey their God.

"[16]Shadrach, Meshach, and Abednego, answered and said to the king, O Nebuchadnezzar, we *are* not careful to answer thee in this matter. [17]If it be *so*, our God whom we serve is able to deliver *us* from the burning fiery furnace, and he will deliver us out of thine hand, O king. [18]But if not, be it known unto thee, O king, that we will not serve thy gods, nor worship the golden image which thou hast set up."
Daniel 3:16-17

The Fiery Furnace

Nebuchadnezzar had Shadrach, Meshach, and Abednego thrown into the fiery furnace and saw, to his surprise, a Christophany. (A pre-incarnate appearance of Christ.)

"[19]Then was Nebuchadnezzar full of fury, and the form of his visage was changed against Shadrach, Meshach, and Abednego: *therefore* he spake, and commanded that they should heat the furnace one seven times more than it was wont to be heated. [20]And he commanded the most mighty men that *were* in his army to bind Shadrach, Meshach, and Abednego, *and* to cast *them* into the burning fiery furnace. [21]Then these men were bound in their coats, their hosen, and their hats, and their *other* garments, and were cast into the midst of the burning fiery furnace. [22]Therefore because the king's commandment was urgent, and the furnace exceeding hot, the flames of the fire slew those men that took up Shadrach, Meshach, and Abednego. [23]And these three men, Shadrach, Meshach, and Abednego, fell down bound into the midst of the burning fiery furnace. [24]Then Nebuchadnezzar the king was astonished, and rose up in haste, *and* spake, and said unto his counsellors, Did not we cast three men bound into the midst of the fire? They answered and said unto the king, True, O king. [25]He answered and said, Lo, I see four men loose, walking in the midst of the fire, and they have no hurt; and the form of the fourth is like **the Son of God**. [26]Then Nebuchadnezzar came near to the mouth of the burning fiery furnace, *and* spake, and said, Shadrach, Meshach, and Abednego, ye servants of the most high God, come forth, and come *hither*. Then Shadrach, Meshach, and Abednego, came forth of the midst of the fire. [27]And the princes, governors, and captains, and the king's counsellors, being gathered together, saw these men, upon whose bodies the fire had no power, nor was an hair of their head singed, neither were their coats changed, nor the smell of fire had passed on them." *Daniel 3:19-27*

Nebuchadnezzar Repents Again

Seeing the work of God again, Nebuchadnezzar repented a second time; but, again, it did not last for long. God's patience will only last so long before He brings judgment.

"²⁸*Then* Nebuchadnezzar spake, and said, Blessed *be* the God of Shadrach, Meshach, and Abednego, who hath sent his angel, and delivered his servants that trusted in him, and have changed the king's word, and yielded their bodies, that they might not serve nor worship any god, except their own God. ²⁹Therefore I make a decree, That every people, nation, and language, which speak any thing amiss against the God of Shadrach, Meshach, and Abednego, shall be cut in pieces, and their houses shall be made a dunghill: because there is no other God that can deliver after this sort. ³⁰Then the king promoted Shadrach, Meshach, and Abednego, in the province of Babylon." *Daniel 3:28-30*

Daniel 3:4-6   The Image of the Beast   Revelation 20:4

Ancient Book of Daniel

Daniel

4

God judged Nebuchadnezzar for his pride. He went insane for seven years. When he came to his senses, he wrote this proclamation:

[1]Nebuchadnezzar the king, unto all people, nations, and languages, that dwell in all the earth; Peace be multiplied unto you. [2]I thought it good to shew the signs and wonders that the high God hath wrought toward me. [3]How great *are* his signs! and how mighty *are* his wonders! his kingdom *is* an everlasting kingdom, and his dominion *is* from generation to generation. [4]I Nebuchadnezzar was at rest in mine house, and flourishing in my palace: [5]I saw a dream which made me afraid, and the thoughts upon my bed and the visions of my head troubled me. [6]Therefore made I a decree to bring in all the wise *men* of Babylon before me, that they might make known unto me the interpretation of the dream. [7]Then came in the magicians, the astrologers, the Chaldeans, and the soothsayers: and I told the dream before them; but they did not make known unto me the interpretation thereof. [8]But at the last Daniel came in before me, whose name *was* Belteshazzar, according to the name of my God, and in whom *is* the spirit of the holy gods: and before him I told the dream, *saying*," Daniel 4:1-8

The Tree Dream

"[9]O Belteshazzar, master of the magicians, because I know that the spirit of the holy gods *is* in thee, and no secret troubleth thee, tell me the visions of my dream that I have seen, and the interpretation thereof. [10]Thus *were* the visions of mine head in my bed; I saw, and behold a tree in the midst of the earth, and the height thereof *was* great. [11]The tree grew, and was strong, and the height thereof reached unto heaven, and the sight thereof to the end of all the earth: [12]The leaves thereof *were* fair, and the fruit thereof much, and in it *was* meat for all: the beasts of the field had shadow under it, and the fowls of the heaven dwelt in the boughs thereof, and all flesh was fed of it. [13]I saw in the visions of my head upon my bed, and, behold, a watcher and an holy one came down from heaven; [14]He cried aloud, and said thus, Hew down the tree, and cut off his branches, shake off his leaves, and scatter his fruit: let the beasts get away from under it, and the fowls from his branches: [15]Nevertheless leave the stump of his roots in the earth, even with a band of iron and brass,[e] in the tender grass of the field; and let it be wet with the dew of heaven, and *let* his portion *be* with the beasts in the grass of the earth: [16]Let his heart be changed from man's, and let a beast's heart be given unto him; and let seven times pass over him. [17]This matter *is* by the decree of the watchers, and the demand by the word of the holy

---

[e] The Hebrew idiom "iron and brass" refers to being protected and remaining strong. See Daniel 7:19 and Psalm 118:8.

ones: to the intent that the living may know that the most High ruleth in the kingdom of men, and giveth it to whomsoever he will, and setteth up over it the basest of men. [18]This dream I king Nebuchadnezzar have seen. Now thou, O Belteshazzar, declare the interpretation thereof, forasmuch as all the wise *men* of my kingdom are not able to make known unto me the interpretation: but thou *art* able; for the spirit of the holy gods *is* in thee." *Daniel 4:9-18*

Daniel's Fear

Daniel was afraid give the interpretation of the dream to King Nebuchadnezzar because the King could command Daniel's execution on the spot.

"[19]Then Daniel, whose name *was* Belteshazzar, was astonied for one hour, and his thoughts troubled him. The king spake, and said, Belteshazzar, let not the dream, or the interpretation thereof, trouble thee. Belteshazzar answered and said, My lord, the dream *be* to them that hate thee, and the interpretation thereof to thine enemies." *Daniel 4:19*

Nebuchadnezzar is the Tree

Daniel explained Nebuchadnezzar himself was that tree because he had expanded his father's Babylonian kingdom to the far reaches of the earth.

"[20]The tree that thou sawest, which grew, and was strong, whose height reached unto the heaven, and the sight thereof to all the earth; [21]Whose leaves *were* fair, and the fruit thereof much, and in it *was* meat for all; under which the beasts of the field dwelt, and upon whose branches the fowls of the heaven had their habitation: [22]It *is* thou, O king, that art grown and become strong: for thy greatness is grown, and reacheth unto heaven, and thy dominion to the end of the earth." *Daniel 4:20-22*

Seven Years of Judgment

Because of Nebuchadnezzar's great pride, God brought a judgment upon him which lasted seven years. Daniel advised Nebuchadnezzar to repent and stay humble and, perhaps, God would show him mercy.

"[23]And whereas the king saw a watcher and an holy one coming down from heaven, and saying, Hew the tree down, and destroy it; yet leave the stump of the roots thereof in the earth, even with a band of iron and brass, in the tender grass of the field; and let it be wet with the dew of heaven, and *let* his portion *be* with the beasts of the field, till seven times pass over him; [24]This *is* the interpretation, O king, and this *is* the decree of the most High, which is come upon my lord the king: [25]That they shall drive thee from men, and thy dwelling shall be with the beasts of the field, and they shall make thee to eat grass as oxen, and they shall wet thee with the dew of heaven, and seven times shall pass over thee, till thou know that the most High ruleth in the kingdom of men, and giveth it to whomsoever he will. [26]And whereas they commanded to leave the stump of the tree roots; thy kingdom shall be sure unto thee, after that thou shalt have known that the heavens do rule. ^{27}Wherefore, O king, let my counsel be acceptable unto thee, and break off thy sins by righteousness, and thine iniquities by shewing mercy to the poor; if it may be a lengthening of thy tranquility." *Daniel 4:23-27*

Jeremiah's Prophecy

Daniel would have known from Jeremiah's prophecy that Nebuchadnezzar, his son, and his grandson would rule Babylon; and in the days of his grandson, the Persians would conquer them. Therefore, Nebuchadnezzar would have to be restored to the throne to have children.

"^{6}And now have I given all these lands into the hand of Nebuchadnezzar the king of Babylon, my servant; and the beasts of the field have I given him also to serve him. ^{7}And all nations shall serve him, and his son, and his son's son, until the very time of his land come: and then many nations and great kings shall serve themselves of him." *Jeremiah 27:6-7*

Nebuchadnezzar's Pride

Nebuchadnezzar's repentance only lasted about a year. Then the prophecy was fulfilled.

"^{28}All this came upon the king Nebuchadnezzar. ^{29}At the end of twelve months he walked in the palace of the kingdom of Babylon. ^{30}The king

spake, and said, Is not this great Babylon, that I have built for the house of the kingdom by the might of my power, and for the honour of my majesty? [31]While the word *was* in the king's mouth, there fell a voice from heaven, *saying*, O king Nebuchadnezzar, to thee it is spoken; The kingdom is departed from thee. [32]And they shall drive thee from men, and thy dwelling *shall be* with the beasts of the field: they shall make thee to eat grass as oxen, and seven times shall pass over thee, until thou know that the most High ruleth in the kingdom of men, and giveth it to whomsoever he will. [33]The same hour was the thing fulfilled upon Nebuchadnezzar: and he was driven from men, and did eat grass as oxen, and his body was wet with the dew of heaven, till his hairs were grown like eagles' *feathers*, and his nails like birds' *claws*."
Daniel 4:28-33

Nebuchadnezzar's Complete Repentance

Nebuchadnezzar finally realized God is in control and does whatever *He* pleases: a lesson we all should learn well.

"[34]And at the end of the days I Nebuchadnezzar lifted up mine eyes unto heaven, and mine understanding returned unto me, and I blessed the most High, and I praised and honoured him that liveth for ever, whose dominion *is* an everlasting dominion, and his kingdom *is* from generation to generation: [35]And all the inhabitants of the earth *are* reputed as nothing: and he doeth according to his will in the army of heaven, and *among* the inhabitants of the earth: and none can stay his hand, or say unto him, What doest thou? [36]At the same time my reason returned unto me; and for the glory of my kingdom, mine honour and brightness returned unto me; and my counsellors and my lords sought unto me; and I was established in my kingdom, and excellent majesty was added unto me. [37]Now I Nebuchadnezzar praise and extol and honour the King of heaven, all whose works *are* truth, and his ways judgment: and those that walk in pride he is able to abase." *Daniel 4:34-37*

Prayer of Nabonidus

Nabonidus is Akkadian for "Nabu is praised." Nabu was the Babylonian god of wisdom. A king named Nabonidus co-ruled with Belshazzar when the Babylonians conquered the kingdom. However, several documents seem to confuse Nabonidus with Nebuchadnezzar. For instance, the Chronicle of Nabonidus stated that he spent seven years in the Tema oasis where Nebuchadnezzar was supposed to have been when he was insane. The document entitled "the Prayer of Nabonidus," Dead Sea scroll 4Q242, has Nabonidus going insane for seven years and being cured by a Jewish prophet.

"Words of the prayer, said by Nabonidus, king of Babylonia, the great king, when afflicted with an ulcer on command of the most high God in Temâ: I, Nabonidus, was afflicted with an evil ulcer for seven years, and far from men I was driven, until I prayed to the most high God. And an exorcist pardoned my sins. He was a Jew from among the children of the exile of Judah, and said: "Recount this in writing to glorify and exalt the name of the most high God." Then I wrote this: "When I was afflicted for seven years by the most high God with an evil ulcer during my stay at Temâ, I prayed to the gods of silver and gold, bronze and iron, wood, stone and lime, because I thought and considered them gods...""" *4Q242*

Sequence of Events

Nebuchadnezzar was told all he needed to know. His kingdom would exist only as long as the Lord saw fit; and it would be in his own best interest to accept the one true God and abandon his paganism.

Daniel, on the other hand, began praying for a more detailed view of future events. When God granted his request, he recorded his visions and their interpretations in chapters 7 and 8. The reader may wish to skip ahead to chapters 7 and 8 and memorize the visions and their interpretations, then return to chapter 5 to see clearly why Daniel acted the way he did.

Daniel
5

Belshazzar, the grandson of Nebuchadnezzar, and the last ruler of the Babylonian Empire as predicted by Jeremiah the prophet, co-ruled Babylon with his step-father Nabonidus[f]. Belshazzar took the sacred vessels stolen from God's temple and used them for a drunken party. He apparently did not believe in the prophecies his grandfather Nebuchadnezzar came to hold dear. Belshazzar had a total disregard for the things of God – an attitude that cost him his life. This should be a serious warning to all of us today.

"[1]Belshazzar the king made a great feast to a thousand of his lords, and drank wine before the thousand. [2]Belshazzar, whiles he tasted the wine, commanded to bring the golden and silver vessels which his father Nebuchadnezzar had taken out of the temple which *was* in Jerusalem; that the king, and his princes, his wives, and his concubines, might drink therein. [3]Then they brought the golden vessels that were taken out of the temple of the house of God which *was* at Jerusalem; and the king, and his princes, his wives, and his concubines, drank in them. [4]They drank wine, and praised the

---

[f] See Who Was Belshazzar at the end of this chapter.

gods of gold, and of silver, of brass, of iron, of wood, and of stone." *Daniel 5:1-4*

The Handwriting on the Wall

God wrote His judgment in the form of a riddle on the wall of Belshazzar's palace. Seeing a disembodied hand writing on the wall scared Belshazzar so badly that his "loins were loosed" and his knees actually knocked together. This was a fulfillment of Isaiah 45:1.

"[1]Thus saith the LORD to his anointed, to Cyrus, whose right hand I have holden, to subdue nations before him; and I will loose the loins of kings, to open before him the two leaved gates; and the gates shall not be shut;" *Isaiah 45:1*

"[5]In the same hour came forth fingers of a man's hand, and wrote over against the candlestick upon the plaister of the wall of the king's palace: and the king saw the part of the hand that wrote. [6]Then the king's countenance was changed, and his thoughts troubled him, so that the joints of his loins were loosed, and his knees smote one against another." *Daniel 5:5-6*

The Coming of Cyrus

To understand why this incident so terrified Belshazzar, we need to understand what Scripture prophesied about Cyrus and the fall of Babylon.

Isaiah wrote his prophecies between 800-700 BC. Centuries before Cyrus was born, Isaiah called him *by name* and prophesied that he would be supernaturally protected by God, allowed to destroy the Babylonian Empire, would free the Jews, and finance the rebuilding of the temple in Jerusalem. Cyrus became king of Persia in 559 BC and conquered Babylon in 537 BC. Isaiah even gave details describing how Cyrus would capture the city of Babylon!

The prediction that the Persians, along with the Medes, would replace the Babylonian Empire is recorded in Isaiah 13:17, 21:2,9 and Daniel 2:39, 5:30-31. Jeremiah prophesied this would occur at the end of the 70 years the Israelites were held captive in Babylon (Jeremiah 25:11-12). The fulfillment is also recorded in Daniel 9:1-3. How did Cyrus accomplish this? Notice Isaiah prophesied Cyrus would dry up or divert a river.

> "[27]That saith to the deep, Be dry, and I will dry up thy rivers: [28]That saith of Cyrus, *He is* my shepherd, and shall perform all my pleasure: even saying to Jerusalem, Thou shalt be built; and to the temple, Thy foundation shall be laid." *Isaiah 44:27-28*

Cyrus besieged Babylon, but could not conquer the city. The city of Babylon had outer walls that were more than seventy feet thick, three hundred feet high, with more than two hundred and fifty watchtowers. It had moats and many other defenses. Since the city sat on the Euphrates River, the inhabitants had all the water and food they needed. They could withstand a siege indefinitely. If Cyrus could not scale the walls or wait them out, how could he conquer the city? Josephus wrote that a group of Jews showed the prophecies to Cyrus. He learned of his destiny and was even told by Isaiah's prophecy how to breach the walls of Babylon!

"[1]Thus saith the LORD to his anointed, to Cyrus, whose right hand I have holden, to subdue nations before him; and I will loose the loins of kings, to open before him the two leaved gates; and the gates shall not be shut; [2]I will go before thee, and make the crooked places straight: I will break in pieces the gates of brass, and cut in sunder the bars of iron: [3]And I will give thee the treasures of darkness, and hidden riches of secret places, that thou mayest know that I, the LORD, which call *thee* by thy name, *am* the God of Israel. [4]For Jacob my servant's sake, and Israel mine elect, I have even called thee by thy name: I have surnamed thee, though thou hast not known me. [5]I *am* the LORD, and *there is* none else, *there is* no God beside me: I girded thee, though thou hast not known me: [6]That they may know from the rising of the sun, and from the west, that *there is* none beside me. I *am* the LORD, and *there is* none else." *Isaiah 45:1-6*

Notice in these two prophecies Isaiah says God would go before Cyrus and open "the gates." He was to command that a river be "dried up." Cyrus took the prophecies literally. Upstream, out of the sight of the Babylonians, his men created a dam and trench that led into a dry river basin. When it was ready, under cover of darkness, he opened the dam and diverted the water into the dry river basin. Cyrus' troops marched quietly down the center of the river *under* the walls of the city. Sure enough, God went before them and caused the brass gates in the water way to be left unlocked. His men entered through the unlocked gates and took the city. The Encyclopedia Judaica records this event occurred on the 14th of Tishrei, the evening before the first day of the Jewish festival of Tabernacles.

The ancient historian Herodotus also recorded the taking of the city by diverting the water. He added that when the dam was opened, the water level of the river dropped

Prophecies Cyrus fulfilled:
Loosed the loins of kings
Freed the Jews
Restored the State of Israel
Funded the Temple's rebuilding
Destroyed Babylonian Empire
Diverted a river and took Babylon

"to the height of the middle of a man's thigh," *Herodotus 1.191.*

The ancient historian Josephus wrote that Cyrus conquered Babylon by believing the literal interpretation of Scripture:

> "'Thus saith Cyrus the king: Since God Almighty hath appointed me to be king of the habitable earth, I believe that he is that God which the nation of the Israelites worship; for indeed he foretold my name by the prophets, and that I should build him a house

at Jerusalem, in the country of Judea.' This was known to Cyrus by his reading the book which Isaiah left behind him of his prophecies; for this prophet said that God had spoken thus to him in a secret vision: 'My will is, that Cyrus, whom I have appointed to be king over many and great nations, send back my people to their own land, and build my temple.' This was foretold by Isaiah one hundred and forty years before the temple was demolished." *Josephus Antiquities 11.1.1-3*

Cyrus' decree to free the Jews and rebuild the Jerusalem Temple is recorded in Ezra 1:1-4. Daniel 5:30 recorded the fall of Babylon. Daniel explained how Darius the Mede[g], under the direction of Cyrus, took control of Babylon. In addition to funding the rebuilding of the Temple, Cyrus also arranged for the sacred vessels from Solomon's Temple to be returned to the Jews. Jeremiah prophesied this and Josephus recorded its fulfillment.

"[19]For thus saith the LORD of hosts concerning the pillars, and concerning the sea, and concerning the bases, and concerning the residue of the vessels that remain in this city. [20]Which Nebuchadnezzar king of Babylon took not, when he carried away captive Jeconiah the son of Jehoiakim king of Judah from Jerusalem to Babylon, and all the nobles of Judah and Jerusalem; [21]Yea, thus saith the LORD of hosts, the God of Israel, concerning the vessels that

---

[g] See Who Was Darius the Mede? at the end of this chapter.

remain *in* the house of the LORD, and *in* the house of the king of Judah and of Jerusalem; [22]They shall be carried to Babylon, and there shall they be until the day that I visit them, saith the LORD; then will I bring them up, and restore them to this place."
Jeremiah 27:19-22

"Upon the rebuilding of their city, and the revival of the ancient practices relating to their worship, Cyrus also sent back to them the vessels of God which King Nebuchadnezzar had pillaged out of the temple, and had carried to Babylon."
Josephus Antiquities 11.1.1-3

Belshazzar Calls for Wise Men

Belshazzar decreed that any wise man who could interpret the handwriting would become third ruler in the Kingdom of Babylon. This was because he was the *second* ruler, while his legal father, Nabonidus, was the *first* ruler in the kingdom. See *Who Was Belshazzar?* at the end of this chapter for complete details. The Queen (his mother, wife of Nabonidus and widow of Evil-Merodach) remembered how accurate Daniel had been in the days of Nebuchadnezzar and recommended that Belshazzar send for him.

"[7]The king cried aloud to bring in the astrologers, the Chaldeans, and the soothsayers. *And* the king spake, and said to the wise *men* of Babylon, Whosoever shall read this writing, and shew me the interpretation thereof, shall be clothed with scarlet, and *have* a chain of gold about his neck, and shall be the third ruler in the kingdom. [8]Then came in all the king's wise *men*: but they could not read the writing, nor make known to the king the interpretation thereof. [9]Then was king Belshazzar greatly troubled, and his countenance was changed in him, and his lords were astonied. [10]*Now* the queen by reason of the words of the king and his lords came into the banquet house: *and* the queen spake and said, O king, live for ever: let not thy thoughts trouble thee, nor let thy countenance be changed: [11]There is a man in thy kingdom, in whom *is* the spirit of the holy gods; and in the days of thy father light and understanding and wisdom, like the wisdom of the gods, was found in him; whom the king Nebuchadnezzar thy father, the king, *I say*, thy father, made master of the magicians, astrologers, Chaldeans, *and* soothsayers; [12]Forasmuch as an excellent spirit, and knowledge, and understanding, interpreting of dreams, and shewing of hard sentences, and dissolving of doubts, were found in the same Daniel, whom the king named Belteshazzar: now let Daniel be called, and he will shew the interpretation." *Daniel 5:7-12*

Daniel Called Before Belshazzar

Belshazzar told Daniel that if he could interpret the writing on the wall, he would make him third ruler in the kingdom. Daniel knew this would be the night the biblical prophecies would be fulfilled and agreed to interpret the writing, but Daniel had no wish to be a ruler when the kingdom would be destroyed in just a few hours.

"¹³Then was Daniel brought in before the king. *And the king spake and said unto Daniel, Art* thou that Daniel, which *art* of the children of the captivity of Judah, whom the king my father brought out of Jewry? ¹⁴I have even heard of thee, that the spirit of the gods *is* in thee, and *that* light and understanding and excellent wisdom is found in thee. ¹⁵And now the wise *men*, the astrologers, have been brought in before me, that they should read this writing, and make known unto me the interpretation thereof: but they could not shew the interpretation of the thing: ¹⁶And I have heard of thee, that thou canst make interpretations, and dissolve doubts: now if thou canst read the writing, and make known to me the interpretation thereof, thou shalt be clothed with scarlet, and *have* a chain of gold about thy neck, and shalt be the third ruler in the kingdom. ¹⁷Then Daniel answered and said before the king, Let thy gifts be to thyself, and give thy rewards to another; yet I will read the writing unto the king, and make known to him the interpretation." *Daniel 5:13-17*

Daniel Reminds Belshazzar of History

Daniel reminded Belshazzar how Nebuchadnezzar was punished because of his pride and his disrespect toward the one true God. Belshazzar showed great disrespect toward that same God by using His sacred vessels for a common feast.

"[18]O thou king, the most high God gave Nebuchadnezzar thy father a kingdom, and majesty, and glory, and honour: [19]And for the majesty that he gave him, all people, nations, and languages, trembled and feared before him: whom he would he slew; and whom he would he kept alive; and whom he would he set up; and whom he would he put down. [20]But when his heart was lifted up, and his mind hardened in pride, he was deposed from his kingly throne, and they took his glory from him: [21]And he was driven from the sons of men; and his heart was made like the beasts, and his dwelling *was* with the wild asses: they fed him with grass like oxen, and his body was wet with the dew of heaven; till he knew that the most high God ruled in the kingdom of men, and *that* he appointeth over it whomsoever he will. [22]And thou his son, O Belshazzar, hast not humbled thine heart, though thou knewest all this; [23]But hast lifted up thyself against the Lord of heaven; and they have brought the vessels of his house before thee, and thou, and thy lords, thy wives, and thy concubines, have drunk wine in them; and thou hast praised the gods of silver, and gold, of brass, iron, wood, and stone, which see not, nor hear, nor know: and the God in whose hand thy breath *is*, and whose *are* all thy ways, hast thou not glorified:" *Daniel 5:18-23*

The Riddle

This riddle of the handwriting on the wall marked both the downfall of the Babylonian Empire and a secondary prophecy for end time Christians to observe: the return to power of the modern state of Israel. See the chapter on timeline prophecies for full details.

"[24]Then was the part of the hand sent from him; and this writing was written. [25]And this *is* the writing that was written, MENE, MENE, TEKEL, UPHARSIN." *Daniel 5:24-25*

מְנֵא

מְנֵא

תְקֵל

וּפַרְסִין

The Interpretation

The Hebrew/Aramaic grammar for the phrase "mena mena tekel upharsin" means "a mena, a mena, a tekel, and a peres." When used as verbs, these words mean: mena, to number; tekel, to weigh; and peres, to divide. Daniel knew all of Isaiah's and Jeremiah's predictions by heart. Since he saw the armies of Cyrus outside Babylon and knew the seventy years ended that very day, he found it very easy to interpret the riddle written on the wall.

"[26]This *is* the interpretation of the thing: MENE; God hath numbered thy kingdom, and finished it. [27]TEKEL; Thou art weighed in the balances, and art found wanting. [28]PERES; Thy kingdom is divided, and given to the Medes and Persians."
Daniel 5:26-28

Daniel's Prediction Fulfilled

That very night, as predicted, the Babylonian Empire fell to the Medes and Persians.

"[29]Then commanded Belshazzar, and they clothed Daniel with scarlet, and *put* a chain of gold about his neck, and made a proclamation concerning him, that he should be the third ruler in the kingdom. [30]In that night was Belshazzar the king of the Chaldeans slain. [31]And Darius the Median took the kingdom, *being* about threescore and two years old."
Daniel 5:29-31

Who was Darius the Mede?

Darius was not a proper name. It was a title of honor that meant "holder of the scepter." According to Persian historical records, a man named Gubaru, a Mede, was appointed by King Cyrus to rule in Babylon. Gubaru was born in 599 BC, making him 62 years old when he invaded Babylon. The exact age is found in Daniel 5:31 and also in the *Ancient Seder Olam.*

"Why does this verse mention Darius was 62 years old? This shows that on the day Nebuchadnezzar entered the Temple of the LORD, when Jehoiachin was reigning in Judah, his arch-enemy Darius was born. The night Belshazzar died and Darius took the kingdom was *exactly* 70 years after Nebuchadnezzar became king of Babylon and 69 years after he conquered Jehoiakim."
Ancient Seder Olam 28

The Descendants of Nebuchadnezzar

Jeremiah predicted the Babylonian Empire would end when the Jews had spent seventy years in captivity. Jeremiah also predicted that the grandson of Nebuchadnezzar would be ruling at that time. Some secular historians say it did not happen that way.

"[6]And now have I given all these lands into the hand of Nebuchadnezzar the king of Babylon, my servant; and the beasts of the field have I given him also to serve him. [7]And all nations shall serve him, and his son, and his son's son, until the very time of his land come: and then many nations and great kings shall serve themselves of him." *Jeremiah 27:6-7*

Who was Belshazzar?

Daniel refers to Nebuchadnezzar as the father of Belshazzar several times in Daniel 5. The word for "father" in Hebrew can also be used for grandfather. According to Jeremiah's prediction[h], Belshazzar had to be the grandson of Nebuchadnezzar, himself. Other Jewish history books also identify him as Nebuchadnezzar's grandson.

> "Nebuchadnezzar reigned 45 years. Evil-Merodach reigned after his father, Nebuchadnezzar, 23 years. Belshazzar reigned after his father, Evil-Merodach, three years."
> *Ancient Seder Olam 28*

Babylonian documents give the following chronology: Nebuchadnezzar ruled for forty-five years (607-562 BC). His son Amel-Marduk (Evil-Merodach) ruled only two years and was assassinated (562-560 BC). The next ruler was the brother-in-law of Nebuchadnezzar, Nergal-shar-usur (560-556 BC). His son, Labashi-Marduk, a grandson of Nebuchadnezzar, ruled only nine months and was assassinated. Then Nabonidus, whose background is not known, took the throne and ruled from 556-537 BC. Nabonidus married one of the widows of Evil-Merodach,

---

[h] Jeremiah 27, see above.

and the crown prince was none other than Belshazzar, the grandson of Nebuchadnezzar.

Nebuchadnezzar (45)	607 – 562 BC
Amel-Marduk (2)	562 – 560 BC
Nergal-shar-usur (4)	560 – 556 BC
Labashi-Marduk	556 BC
Nabonidus (19)	556 – 537 BC
Belshazzar (co-ruler with Nabonidus)	540 – 537 BC

Evidently the Ancient Seder Olam counted the reign of Evil-Merodach and his widow's as one rule until his son, Belshazzar, took the throne. It refused to count any non-male descendant of Nebuchadnezzar. This would also explain why Belshazzar could only make Daniel the third ruler in the kingdom according to verse 16; Belshazzar was second ruler, while Nebonidus was the first.

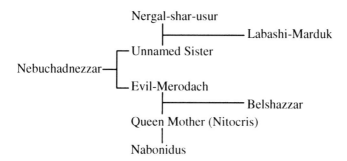

Ancient Book of Daniel

Daniel
6

This chapter records events that took place after 537 BC, when the Medes and Persians were ruling Babylon.

"¹It pleased Darius to set over the kingdom an hundred and twenty princes, which should be over the whole kingdom; ²And over these three presidents; of whom Daniel *was* first: that the princes might give accounts unto them, and the king should have no damage. ³Then this Daniel was preferred above the presidents and princes, because an excellent spirit *was* in him; and the king thought to set him over the whole realm." *Daniel 6:1-3*

When you stand up for God, the ungodly will try to find ways to persecute you.

"⁴Then the presidents and princes sought to find occasion against Daniel concerning the kingdom; but they could find none occasion nor fault; forasmuch as he *was* faithful, neither was there any error or fault found in him. ⁵Then said these men, We shall not find any occasion against this Daniel, except we find *it* against him concerning the law of his God. ⁶Then these presidents and princes assembled together to the king, and said thus unto him, King Darius, live for ever. ⁷All the presidents

of the kingdom, the governors, and the princes, the counsellors, and the captains, have consulted together to establish a royal statute, and to make a firm decree, that whosoever shall ask a petition of any God or man for thirty days, save of thee, O king, he shall be cast into the den of lions."
Daniel 6:4-7

Persian Decrees

I believe the main reason for including this chapter is to show that once a Persian king made a decree, the decree could not be changed or abolished, even by the king. In contrast, in Babylon the king was completely sovereign; he could change any decree he wished. A Babylonian king could simply change his mind and change or abolish a decree he just made.[i]

This goes back to what Daniel taught about Nebuchadnezzar's image with the ten toes. Babylon, the golden head, was rare and the government completely sovereign. The silver chest, Persia, was less sovereign. The Roman Empire fell after it was split in two. The ten nations will be completely ineffective because of their confederacy. When the Antichrist takes them over, he *will* be effective because he will become a dictator like Nebuchadnezzar of Babylon was.

[8]Now, O king, establish the decree, and sign the writing, that it be not changed, according to the law

---

[i] Esther 8:8 also shows once a Persian law is decreed, it cannot be altered.

of the Medes and Persians, which altereth not.
⁹Wherefore king Darius signed the writing and the
decree." *Daniel 6:8-9*

Daniel Followed God Not Men

Even though Daniel knew his daily prayers were now
illegal, he continued to pray in spite of the new law.
Today some Christians will not even pray before eating
their lunch at work, because it might offend a coworker or
they might actually be laughed at. We should be ashamed.
Daniel accepted his trial just as Shadrach, Meshach, and
Abednego accepted theirs, concluding that it must be
God's will for a greater witness later.

"¹⁰Now when Daniel knew that the writing was
signed, he went into his house; and his windows
being open in his chamber toward Jerusalem, he
kneeled upon his knees three times a day, and
prayed, and gave thanks before his God, as he did
aforetime. ¹¹Then these men assembled, and found
Daniel praying and making supplication before his
God. ¹²Then they came near, and spake before the
king concerning the king's decree; Hast thou not
signed a decree, that every man that shall ask *a
petition* of any God or man within thirty days, save
of thee, O king, shall be cast into the den of lions?
The king answered and said, The thing *is* true,
according to the law of the Medes and Persians,
which altereth not. ¹³Then answered they and said
before the king, That Daniel, which *is* of the
children of the captivity of Judah, regardeth not

thee, O king, nor the decree that thou hast signed, but maketh his petition three times a day. [14]Then the king, when he heard *these* words, was sore displeased with himself, and set *his* heart on Daniel to deliver him: and he laboured till the going down of the sun to deliver him." *Daniel 6:10-14*

Darius could not change the decree, but spent the night fasting and praying for Daniel.

"[15]Then these men assembled unto the king, and said unto the king, Know, O king, that the law of the Medes and Persians *is*, That no decree nor statute which the king established may be changed. [16]Then the king commanded, and they brought Daniel, and cast *him* into the den of lions. *Now* the king spake and said unto Daniel, Thy God whom thou servest continually, he will deliver thee. [17]And a stone was brought, and laid upon the mouth of the den; and the king sealed it with his own signet, and with the signet of his lords; that the purpose might not be changed concerning Daniel. [18]Then the king went to his palace, and passed the night fasting: neither were instruments of musick brought before him: and his sleep went from him." *Daniel 6:15-18*

The Angel Protects Daniel

God always has ways of protecting His people and achieving what He desires. Since God had plans for Daniel, he could not be killed before his time. It is the same with us. Once we have finished the work God has for us, then – and only then – can we be killed. We should have the same attitude Paul had when he said, "To live is Christ, but to die is gain."

"¹⁹Then the king arose very early in the morning, and went in haste unto the den of lions. ²⁰And when he came to the den, he cried with a lamentable voice unto Daniel: *and* the king spake and said to Daniel, O Daniel, servant of the living God, is thy God, whom thou servest continually, able to deliver thee from the lions? ²¹Then said Daniel unto the king, O king, live for ever. ²²My God hath sent his angel, and hath shut the lions' mouths, that they have not hurt me: forasmuch as before him innocency was found in me; and also before thee, O king, have I done no hurt. ²³Then was the king exceedingly glad for him, and commanded that they should take Daniel up out of the den. So Daniel was taken up out of the den, and no manner of hurt was found upon him, because he believed in his God." *Daniel 6:19-23*

The Pagans Punished

Those who persecute Christians will ultimately suffer for it. God may allow them to prosper for a time, but unless they repent, they will parish.

"²⁴And the king commanded, and they brought those men which had accused Daniel, and they cast *them* into the den of lions, them, their children, and their wives; and the lions had the mastery of them, and brake all their bones in pieces or ever they came at the bottom of the den. [25]Then king Darius wrote unto all people, nations, and languages, that dwell in all the earth; Peace be multiplied unto you. [26]I make a decree, That in every dominion of my kingdom men tremble and fear before the God of Daniel: for he is the living God, and steadfast for ever, and his kingdom *that* which shall not be destroyed, and his dominion *shall be even* unto the end. [27]He delivereth and rescueth, and he worketh signs and wonders in heaven and in earth, who hath delivered Daniel from the power of the lions." *Daniel 6:24-27*

Daniel's Long Life

As we learned earlier, Daniel was a young man when taken to Babylon with the first wave of captives, in 606 BC. The Scriptures tell us that he continued ruling in Babylon under Darius and Cyrus, which was past 536 BC. Daniel lived well over eighty years.

"[28]So this Daniel prospered in the reign of Darius, and in the reign of Cyrus the Persian." *Daniel 6:28*

Daniel
7

The four Great Beasts

This chapter records the visions God gave Daniel in the first year of the reign of Belshazzar, about 540 BC. God gave Daniel more detail about the four kingdoms represented by Nebuchadnezzar's great image described in chapter 2.

"¹In the first year of Belshazzar king of Babylon Daniel had a dream and visions of his head upon his bed: then he wrote the dream, *and* told the sum of the matters. ²Daniel spake and said, I saw in my vision by night, and, behold, the four winds of the heaven strove upon the great sea. ³And four great beasts came up from the sea, diverse one from another." *Daniel 7:1-3*

The Lion – Babylon

The winged lion represented the Babylonian Empire which ruled over the Jews for seventy years, 607-537 BC. The winged lion corresponds to the golden head of Nebuchadnezzar's image. The wings being plucked and a man's heart being given to it reminds us that when Nebuchadnezzar regained his sanity, he worshiped the one true God.

"⁴The first *was* like a lion, and had eagle's wings: I beheld till the wings thereof were plucked, and it was lifted up from the earth, and made stand upon the feet as a man, and a man's heart was given to it."
Daniel 7:4

The Bear – Persia

The bear with one side higher than the other represented the combined empire of the Medes and Persians. This beast corresponds to the chest and arms of silver. Babylon, in fear of Cyrus, formed a coalition with the kingdoms of Egypt and Lydia. These are represented by the three ribs in the bear's mouth, which proved to be no match for the armies of Cyrus. Lydia fell to the Persians in 544 BC; Babylon, in 537 BC; and Egypt, in 523 BC.

"⁵And behold another beast, a second, like to a bear, and it raised up itself on one side, and *it had* three ribs in the mouth of it between the teeth of it: and they said thus unto it, Arise, devour much flesh."
Daniel 7:5

The Leopard - Greece

The leopard represented the kingdom of Greece led by Alexander the Great. Greece conquered the Medio-Persian Empire in 323 BC. Shortly after

Alexander's death, his kingdom split into four parts, each led by a general from his army. All this, and more, is described in detail in chapter 11. This beast corresponds to the belly and thighs of brass. The four wings represent the lightening speed by which Alexander conquered the Middle East.

> "⁶After this I beheld, and lo another, like a leopard, which had upon the back of it four wings of a fowl; the beast had also four heads; and dominion was given to it." *Daniel 7:6*

Terrible Beast – Rome

The fourth beast is not described but is stronger than all that came before it (controlled more territory). This was Rome and corresponds to the legs of iron. We know this was Rome both from history and from Daniel 11:30 where it mentions the ships coming from "Chittim" (the Hebrew word for Rome).

> "⁷After this I saw in the night visions, and behold a fourth beast, dreadful and terrible, and strong exceedingly; and it had great iron teeth: it devoured and brake in pieces, and stamped the residue with the feet of it: and it *was* diverse from all the beasts that *were* before it; and it had ten horns." *Daniel 7:7*

The Ten Horns

The ten horns[j] correspond to the ten toes on Nebuchadnezzar's great image. We learned in chapter 2 that the Roman Empire was prophesied to be divided, then fall. These two events occurred in AD  325 and 476. Sometime later, out of what was the Roman Empire, the ten-kingdom confederacy would form. This part of the prophecy is yet future. Now God gives us new information. After the ten kingdoms form their alliance, another kingdom arises, headed by what Christians call the Antichrist. In trying to take over the ten-kingdom confederacy, three of the kingdoms rebel and the Antichrist destroys them. We will see in chapter 11 that one of the three nations that rebel against the Antichrist will be Egypt.

> "[8]I considered the horns, and, behold, there came up among them another little horn, before whom there were three of the first horns plucked up by the roots: and, behold, in this horn *were* eyes like the eyes of man, and a mouth speaking great things."
> *Daniel 7:8*

Day of Judgment

God will pass judgment on the Antichrist and kill him.

---

[j] The ancient church taught the ten horns are a end-time revived Roman Empire. See Appendix A.

"[9]I beheld till the thrones were cast down, and the Ancient of days did sit, whose garment *was* white as snow, and the hair of his head like the pure wool: his throne *was like* the fiery flame, *and* his wheels *as* burning fire. [10]A fiery stream issued and came forth from before him: thousand thousands ministered unto him, and ten thousand times ten thousand stood before him: the judgment was set, and the books were opened. [11]I beheld then because of the voice of the great words which the horn spake: I beheld *even* till the beast was slain, and his body destroyed, and given to the burning flame." *Daniel 7:9-11*

The phrase "cast down" refers to the thrones descending from heaven and being set up for judgment, not that they were defeated in some way. The remnants of the empires of Babylon, Persia, Greece, and Rome still exist today as the countries of Iraq (Babylon), Iran (Persia), Greece, and Rome/Italy. They never regained any semblance of empire stature again; but, as prophesied, they still exist!

"[12]As concerning the rest of the beasts, they had their dominion taken away: yet their lives were prolonged for a season and time." *Daniel 7:12*

The Messianic Kingdom
After the destruction of the Antichrist, the Messiah will set up a millennial reign. Revelation 20:4 reveals the Messiah's reign will last for one thousand years.

"[13]I saw in the night visions, and, behold, *one* like the Son of man came with the clouds of heaven, and came to the Ancient of days, and they brought him near before him. [14]And there was given him dominion, and glory, and a kingdom, that all people, nations, and languages, should serve him: his dominion *is* an everlasting dominion, which shall not pass away, and his kingdom *that* which shall not be destroyed." *Daniel 7:13-14*

The Interpretation

Daniel is told the beasts represent the four empires. After their rule, will come the eternal kingdom of the Messiah. Daniel also reveals that the Antichrist will make war with the saints and *overcome* them. Since this was written in Daniel's day, long before there were Christians, the word "saints" refer to the Jews. See verse 25 for proof.

"[15]I Daniel was grieved in my spirit in the midst of *my* body, and the visions of my head troubled me. [16]I came near unto one of them that stood by, and asked him the truth of all this. So he told me, and made me know the interpretation of the things. [17]These great beasts, which are four, *are* four kings, *which* shall arise out of the earth. [18]But the saints of the most High shall take the kingdom, and possess the kingdom for ever, even for ever and ever. [19]Then I would know the truth of the fourth beast, which was diverse from all the others, exceeding dreadful, whose teeth *were of* iron, and his nails *of*

brass;[k] *which* devoured, brake in pieces, and stamped the residue with his feet; [20]And of the ten horns that *were* in his head, and *of* the other which came up, and before whom three fell; even *of* that horn that had eyes, and a mouth that spake very great things, whose look *was* more stout than his fellows. [21]I beheld, and the same horn made war with the saints, and prevailed against them; [22]Until the Ancient of days came, and judgment was given to the saints of the most High; and the time came that the saints possessed the kingdom."
Daniel 7:15-22

The Antichrist's Kingdom

In this section the Scriptures foretell that the Antichrist will change times and laws. In Daniel 9:27 we will learn that the Antichrist will stop temple sacrifices. He will exercise complete control over the Jews for three and a half years. We will learn about his rise to power in chapters 9 and 11, which will show this will all take place over a seven-year period right before the Second Coming of Jesus Christ to earth.

"[23]Thus he said, The fourth beast shall be the fourth kingdom upon earth, which shall be diverse from all kingdoms, and shall devour the whole earth, and shall tread it down, and break it in pieces. [24]And the ten horns out of this kingdom *are* ten kings *that* shall arise: and another shall rise after them; and he

---

[k] The Hebrew idiom "iron and brass" refers to being protected and remaining strong. See Daniel 4:15 and Psalm 118:8.

shall be diverse from the first, and he shall subdue three kings. [25]And he shall speak *great* words against the most High, and shall wear out the saints of the most High, and think to change times and laws: and they shall be given into his hand until a time and times and the dividing of time. [26]But the judgment shall sit, and they shall take away his dominion, to consume and to destroy *it* unto the end. [27]And the kingdom and dominion, and the greatness of the kingdom under the whole heaven, shall be given to the people of the saints of the most High, whose kingdom *is* an everlasting kingdom, and all dominions shall serve and obey him." *Daniel 7:23-27*

"Speaking great words against the Most High" probably refers to the Antichrist claiming to be God incarnate and denying Jesus Christ. We will learn more details about these things in chapter 11.

Daniel's Distress

It upset Daniel to discover that several empires would rule over the Jews before the final reign of the Messiah. However, he believed the prophecies were literal and he continued to ponder them.

"[28]Hitherto *is* the end of the matter. As for me Daniel, my cogitations much troubled me, and my countenance changed in me: but I kept the matter in my heart." *Daniel 7:28*

Note on Cults

Cultic groups like the Seventh Day Adventists, among others, have taught that in addition to these beasts representing Babylon, Persia, Greece, and Rome; they also represent modern nations like the USA, Russia, Great Britain, and China. While there are both double fulfillment prophecies and dual purpose prophecies, some of which are given in this book, this vision of the beasts has only one interpretation. None of these countries ever conquered one of the other three. The USA came out of Great Britain, but none of the others were born out of the remaining three countries.

A mature Christian can usually recognize something is just not right when listening to a cultic group reinventing prophecy.

Ancient Book of Daniel

Daniel

8

In the same year Belshazzar died and Babylon was conquered by the Persian armies of Cyrus, God revealed more prophetic insights to Daniel. Daniel knew Babylon was about to fall to Persia because of the prophecies in the books of Jeremiah and Isaiah, but he still pondered which countries would be the third and fourth kingdoms. He also wanted to know more about this end time kingdom that would exist when the Messiah set up His kingdom.

"¹In the third year of the reign of king Belshazzar a vision appeared unto me, *even unto* me Daniel, after that which appeared unto me at the first. ²And I saw in a vision; and it came to pass, when I saw, that I *was* at Shushan *in* the palace, which *is* in the province of Elam; and I saw in a vision, and I was by the river of Ulai." *Daniel 8:1 -2*

The Ram – Symbol of Persia
The ram was the national symbol of Persia.

"³Then I lifted up mine eyes, and saw, and, behold, there stood before the river a ram which had *two* horns: and the *two* horns *were* high; but one *was* higher than the other, and the higher came up last. ⁴I saw the ram pushing westward, and northward, and southward; so that no beasts might stand before him, neither *was there any* that could deliver out of his hand; but he did according to his will, and became great." *Daniel 8:3-4*

In this vision, one horn was higher than the other, just like one side of the bear in chapter 7 was higher than the other. This ram symbolized the Medio-Persian Empire. Persia was the more powerful (or higher part) of the two kingdoms.

The Goat – Symbol of Greece

A goat was the national symbol of Greece and represented the same empire as the four-headed leopard of chapter 8.

"[5]And as I was considering, behold, an he goat came from the west on the face of the whole earth, and touched not the ground: and the goat *had* a notable horn between his eyes. [6]And he came to the ram that had *two* horns, which I had seen standing before the river, and ran unto him in the fury of his power. [7]And I saw him come close unto the ram, and he was moved with choler against him, and smote the ram, and brake his two horns: and there was no power in the ram to stand before him, but he cast him down to the ground, and stamped upon him: and there was none that could deliver the ram out of his hand." *Daniel 8:5-7*

The notable horn represented Alexander the Great who conquered Persia. Daniel 11:2 describes how a Persian king would attack Greece and Alexander would seek revenge. He would be "moved with choler" or extremely angry and would be so swift in his attack that he "touched not the ground" when he came against Persia. This prophecy was fulfilled when Alexander defeated the troops of Darius at Hellespont in 334 BC.

Alexander the Great

Josephus, in his *Antiquities 11.8.3-7*, described how Alexander came to Jerusalem. He related that Alexander came into Syria and captured first Damascus, then Sidon, and finally besieged Tyre for seven months. He sent word to the high priest of Jerusalem demanding supplies for his troops. But the high priest, Jaddua, refused, saying he was under obligation to Darius of Persia and could not help. After Alexander destroyed Tyre, he proceeded south along the border and conquered all of Gaza.

After these conquests, Alexander came to besiege Jerusalem, put the high priest to death for disobedience, and sack the temple for gold. God warned the high priest in a dream not to resist Alexander. When the high priest saw Alexander's army approaching, he opened the gates and sent out the priests in white robes in two rows. Then he went out to meet Alexander in front of the procession. When Alexander saw the high priest, he realized that he had seen this man with the breastplate of crystals in a dream. In his dream, the high priest told him he would subjugate Persia. So Alexander respectfully greeted the high priest and made a sacrifice to God as Gentiles do. The high priest then showed Alexander the prophecies recorded in Daniel 8 and 11. Daniel prophesied that the fourth Persian king, after Cyrus, would attack Greece, which had already been fulfilled by that time. After this attack on Greece, a mighty Greek king would rise up and defeat the Persians (see Daniel 11:3). Alexander believed the prophecies and went on to conquer the Persian Empire.

The Antichrist

When Alexander died, his kingdom was split into four smaller kingdoms: Egypt, Syria, Macedonia (Greece), and Thrace (part of modern day Turkey).[1]

"[8]Therefore the he goat waxed very great: and when he was strong, the great horn was broken; and for it came up four notable ones toward the four winds of heaven. [9]And out of one of them came forth a little horn, which waxed exceeding great, toward the

---

[1] See Daniel 11:3-4 for details.

south, and toward the east, and toward the pleasant *land.*" *Daniel 8:8-9*

In this dream Daniel learned that the future Antichrist, the eleventh horn, would rule one of Alexander's four kingdoms. Daniel 11:40 explained that the Antichrist is the king of the north and will attack Egypt, the king of the south. In doing so, his empire would spread south, east, and toward Israel. So the Antichrist will come from a country north of Israel, probably Lebanon, Syria, or Iraq.

The Antichrist will demand that his subjects worship him as God. This is the same way Lucifer wanted to be worshiped as God by the angels when he caused the rebellion and fall of one third of the angels.

"[10]And it waxed great, *even* to the host of heaven; and it cast down *some* of the host and of the stars to the ground, and stamped upon them. [11]Yea, he magnified *himself* even to the prince of the host, and by him the daily *sacrifice* was taken away, and the place of the sanctuary was cast down. [12]And an host was given *him* against the daily *sacrifice* by reason of transgression, and it cast down the truth to the ground; and it practised, and prospered." *Daniel 8:10-12*

"[22]Who is a liar but he that denieth that Jesus is the Christ? He is antichrist, that denieth the Father and the Son." *1 John 2:22*

The Antichrist will claim to be greater than the "prince of the host," or Jesus Christ. The apostle John taught the Antichrist will teach Jesus was not the *only* Christ. He will claim he is God incarnate, not Jesus, denying Jesus' unique relationship with the Father. Daniel 9 gives more detail by saying the Antichrist will stop the temple sacrifices and defile the sanctuary in the Jerusalem temple. The Antichrist will defile the temple by placing an image (or teraphim) in the temple. He will "cast truth to the ground" by preaching his weird occult religion. See chapters 9 and 11 for details.

2300 Days

"[13]Then I heard one saint speaking, and another saint said unto that certain *saint* which spake, How long *shall be* the vision *concerning* the daily *sacrifice*, and the transgression of desolation, to give both the sanctuary and the host to be trodden under foot? [14]And he said unto me, Unto two thousand and three hundred days; then shall the sanctuary be cleansed. [15]And it came to pass, when I, *even* I Daniel, had seen the vision, and sought for the meaning, then, behold, there stood before me as the appearance of a man. [16]And I heard a man's voice between *the banks of* Ulai,[m] which called, and said, Gabriel, make this *man* to understand the vision." *Daniel 8:13-17*

---

[m] The Ulai River flowed from Shushan, the capital of Persia.

Some have taught the 2,300 days of verse 14 refers to the time Antiochus IV Epiphanies defiled the temple back in 165 BC. However, the angel Gabriel clearly revealed that this period refers to the end-time empire of the Antichrist. The 2,300 days will begin when the Abomination of Desolation is set up in the middle of the seven-year Tribulation, and ends when the foundation stone is laid for the millennial temple just after the start of the one-thousand-year reign of Jesus Christ. See chapter 12 for details on how the 1260 days, 1290 days, 1335 days and the 2300 days fit together.

Seven-year Tribulation

"[17]So he came near where I stood: and when he came, I was afraid, and fell upon my face: but he said unto me, Understand, O son of man: for at the time of the end *shall be* the vision. [18]Now as he was speaking with me, I was in a deep sleep on my face toward the ground: but he touched me, and set me upright. [19]And he said, Behold, I will make thee know what shall be in the last end of the indignation: for at the time appointed the end *shall be*." *Daniel 8:17-19*

We do not learn the Tribulation period will last for seven years until chapter 9; but Daniel had already revealed to us that it will end with the coming of the Messianic kingdom. Here it is called "the indignation." This title is used by Isaiah (26:20) and other prophets to describe the last days.

Persia, Greece, and Alexander

> "[20]The ram which thou sawest having *two* horns *are* the kings of Media and Persia. [21]And the rough goat *is* the king of Grecia: and the great horn that *is* between his eyes *is* the first king." *Daniel 8:20-21*

The angel Gabriel explained to Daniel that the ram represents Persia; and the goat, Greece, and the notable horn on the goat is the first king, Alexander the Great. The angel Gabriel gave this prediction more than 250 years before Alexander the Great was born!

The Four Grecian Kingdoms

We already know that Alexander the Great's empire broke into four smaller empires: Greece, Syria, Egypt, and Turkey. This will be detailed in chapter 11. In AD 1299, Turkey created the great Ottoman Empire and conquered Syria, Egypt, Greece, and many other nations. The Ottoman Empire lasted from AD 1299 to 1923.

> "[22]Now that being broken, whereas four stood up for it, four kingdoms shall stand up out of the nation, but not in his power. [23]And in the latter time of their kingdom, when the transgressors are come to the full, a king of fierce countenance, and

understanding dark sentences, shall stand up."
Daniel 8:22-23

Since Daniel wrote that in the later days, when the Antichrist rises to power, these four nations would be ruling independently, the Ottoman Empire *had* to be dissolved and these ancient nations recreated and given their independence. The Ottoman Empire came to an end in WWI. After WWI, Syria, Egypt, and Turkey were recreated by the League of Nations. Egypt became autonomous in 1922, Turkey in 1929, and Syria in 1944. Greece was conquered by the Ottoman Empire in AD 1453, but managed to break away, gaining its independence in 1829. Over the next century it regained its former islands, but was conquered again by the Nazis during WWII. After WWII, the nationalists and communists waged a civil war. By 1975 a democratic government was firmly in place and continues to this day.

The rise of Antichrist must occur after these four regain their independence, (in AD 1944) and after the "the transgressors have run their course." I believe this refers to the persecution of the Jews during the great dispersion, which ended with the Holocaust. The Holocaust set the stage for the return if the nation of Israel. They will not be conquered again until the raise of the Antichrist.

To date, the Holocaust has been the worst catastrophe the Jews have ever faced, including the destruction of the Temple in AD 70. We can safely say to preterists that the Tribulation did not occur in AD 70.

Details About the Antichrist

The Antichrist will be the most powerful person in his time, but not because of human effort or armies, but because of demonic forces. He will persecute and destroy the Israelis. He cannot be killed or stopped by human effort, but only by the return of Jesus Christ to earth.

> "[24]And his power shall be mighty, but not by his own power: and he shall destroy wonderfully, and shall prosper, and practise, and shall destroy the mighty and the holy people. [25]And through his policy also he shall cause craft to prosper in his hand; and he shall magnify *himself* in his heart, and by peace shall destroy many: he shall also stand up against the Prince of princes; but he shall be broken without hand." *Daniel 8:24-25*

Although Daniel trusted God for everything, these visions upset him so much he became physically ill. Daniel, Shadrach, Meshach, and Abednego collectively tried to compare all these visions with the writings of the Old Testament prophets; but, they could not completely understand them.

> "[26]And the vision of the evening and the morning which was told *is* true: wherefore shut thou up the vision; for it *shall be* for many days. [27]And I Daniel fainted, and was sick *certain* days; afterward I rose up, and did the king's business; and I was astonished at the vision, but none understood *it*." *Daniel 8:26-27*

Daniel
9

The Isaiah and Jeremiah Prophecies Fulfilled

In 536 BC, the year Cyrus and Darius took over Babylon, Daniel realized the prophecies of Isaiah and Jeremiah had literally been fulfilled.

> ¹In the first year of Darius the son of Ahasuerus, of the seed of the Medes, which was made king over the realm of the Chaldeans; ²In the first year of his reign I Daniel understood by books the number of the years, whereof the word of the LORD came to Jeremiah the prophet, that he would accomplish seventy years in the desolations of Jerusalem."
> *Daniel 9:1-2*

After the children of Israel had forsaken Him, the Lord decreed their punishment through Jeremiah the prophet. Nebuchadnezzar would take them captive for seventy years.

> "And this whole land shall be a desolation, *and* an astonishment; and these nations shall serve the king of Babylon seventy years. And it shall come to pass, when seventy years are accomplished, *that* I will punish the king of Babylon, and that nation, saith the LORD, for their iniquity, and the land of the

Chaldeans, and will make it perpetual desolations."
Jeremiah 25:11-12

The prophet Isaiah predicted that a coalition of Medes and Persians would destroy Babylon. Isaiah even prophesied their leader would be named Cyrus and told exactly how he would conquer the city of Babylon. See chapter 5 for details on Cyrus and the taking of Babylon.

"Behold, I will stir up the Medes against them, which shall not regard silver; and *as for* gold, they shall not delight in it." *Isaiah 13:17*

"That saith of Cyrus, *He is* my shepherd, and shall perform all my pleasure: even saying to Jerusalem, Thou shalt be built; and to the temple, Thy foundation shall be laid." *Isaiah 44:28*

Daniel's Prayer of Repentance and Thanksgiving

Even though Daniel believed the prophecies would be fulfilled no matter what, he still humbly pleaded for the Lord to fulfill them. He was not arrogant enough to *demand* that God fulfill His promises. He also recognized that we have all personally sinned before the Lord and humbly asked forgiveness in all these areas. This attitude is what it takes to be a mature Christian. A mature Christian will never try to command God to do something or try to argue with Him in order to get something. Instead, a mature Christian is willing to accept whatever God's will is for his life.

"[3]And I set my face unto the Lord God, to seek by prayer and supplications, with fasting,[n] and sackcloth, and ashes: [4]And I prayed unto the LORD my God, and made my confession, and said, O Lord, the great and dreadful God, keeping the covenant and mercy to them that love him, and to them that keep his commandments; [5]We have sinned, and have committed iniquity, and have done wickedly, and have rebelled, even by departing from thy precepts and from thy judgments: [6]Neither have we hearkened unto thy servants the prophets, which spake in thy name to our kings, our princes, and our fathers, and to all the people of the land. [7]O LORD, righteousness *belongeth* unto thee, but unto us confusion of faces, as at this day; to the men of Judah, and to the inhabitants of Jerusalem, and unto all Israel, *that are* near, and *that are* far off, through all the countries whither thou hast driven them, because of their trespass that they have trespassed against thee. [8]O Lord, to us *belongeth* confusion of face, to our kings, to our princes, and to our fathers, because we have sinned against thee. [9]To the Lord our God *belong* mercies and forgivenesses, though we have rebelled against him; [10]Neither have we obeyed the voice of the LORD our God, to walk in his laws, which he set before us by his servants the prophets. [11]Yea, all Israel have transgressed thy law, even by departing, that they might not obey thy voice; therefore the curse is poured upon us, and the

---

[n] Jews were required to fast on the Festival of Yom Kippur. See the chapter on *The Fall Festivals* for its prophetic significance.

oath that *is* written in the law of Moses the servant of God, because we have sinned against him. [12]And he hath confirmed his words, which he spake against us, and against our judges that judged us, by bringing upon us a great evil: for under the whole heaven hath not been done as hath been done upon Jerusalem. [13]As *it is* written in the law of Moses, all this evil is come upon us: yet made we not our prayer before the LORD our God, that we might turn from our iniquities, and understand thy truth. [14]Therefore hath the LORD watched upon the evil, and brought it upon us: for the LORD our God *is* righteous in all his works which he doeth: for we obeyed not his voice. [15]And now, O Lord our God, that hast brought thy people forth out of the land of Egypt with a mighty hand, and hast gotten thee renown, as at this day; we have sinned, we have done wickedly. [16]O LORD, according to all thy righteousness, I beseech thee, let thine anger and thy fury be turned away from thy city Jerusalem, thy holy mountain: because for our sins, and for the iniquities of our fathers, Jerusalem and thy people *are become* a reproach to all *that are* about us. [17]Now therefore, O our God, hear the prayer of thy servant, and his supplications, and cause thy face to shine upon thy sanctuary that is desolate, for the Lord's sake. [18]O my God, incline thine ear, and hear; open thine eyes, and behold our desolations, and the city which is called by thy name: for we do not present our supplications before thee for our righteousnesses, but for thy great mercies. [19]O Lord,

hear; O Lord, forgive; O Lord, hearken and do; defer not, for thine own sake, O my God: for thy city and thy people are called by thy name."
Daniel 9:3-19

The Angel Gabriel Arrived

The angel Gabriel appeared to Daniel to teach him about the first coming of the Messiah and other things that would accompany this great event. Would it not be amazing to not only have an angel appear to us to teach us about God's ways, but to actually state we are well known and greatly loved in heaven? If we set our hearts to understand prophecy and follow God's will for our lives, that just might take place.

"²⁰And whiles I *was* speaking, and praying, and confessing my sin and the sin of my people Israel, and presenting my supplication before the LORD my God for the holy mountain of my God; ²¹Yea, whiles I *was* speaking in prayer, even the man Gabriel, whom I had seen in the vision at the beginning, being caused to fly swiftly, touched me about the time of the evening oblation.° ²²And he informed *me*, and talked with me, and said, O Daniel, I am now come forth to give thee skill and understanding. ²³At the beginning of thy supplications the commandment came forth, and I

° The evening oblation is a temple sacrifice that occurs at 3:PM. On Yom Kippur this would be the time for the scapegoat ritual. See the chapter on *The Fall Festivals* for its prophetic significance.

am come to shew *thee*; for thou *art* greatly beloved: therefore understand the matter, and consider the vision." *Daniel 9:20-23*

The Prophecy of the Seventy Weeks

Daniel fully understood Jeremiah's prophecy about the seventy-year captivity. The angel Gabriel came to reveal *another* prophecy, one about seventy *weeks* of years.

> "[24]Seventy weeks are determined upon thy people and upon thy holy city, to finish the transgression, and to make an end of sins, and to make reconciliation for iniquity, and to bring in everlasting righteousness, and to seal up the vision and prophecy, and to anoint the most Holy."
> *Daniel 9:24*

There are seven days in a week, so seventy weeks of years would be seventy times seven or 490 years. Gabriel explained that there would be seventy weeks of years between the time a decree was given to rebuild the city of Jerusalem and the advent of the messianic kingdom. Then the Messiah, or "Holy One," would be crowned king of the earth.

AD 32

The angel Gabriel predicted that from the decree to rebuild Jerusalem until the Messiah would be seven weeks plus another sixty-two weeks. During the first seven weeks (forty nine years) the wall of the city of Jerusalem and the city itself would be rebuilt.

"²⁵Know therefore and understand, *that* from the going forth of the commandment to restore and to build Jerusalem unto the Messiah the Prince *shall be* seven weeks, and threescore and two weeks: the street shall be built again, and the wall, even in troublous times. ²⁶And after threescore and two weeks shall Messiah be cut off, but not for himself:" *Daniel 9:25*

Nehemiah 2:1 recorded that the decree to restore and rebuild Jerusalem occurred in the month of Nissan in the twentieth year of the reign of the Persian king, Artaxerxes. Encyclopedia Britannica gives the date Artaxerxes Longimanus took the Persian throne as July of 465 BC. Therefore, his twentieth year began in July of 445 BC. The month of Nissan following that would have been in March of 444 BC, which occurred before the twenty-first anniversary of Artaxerxes' reign. The seven weeks, or forty-nine years, ran from Artaxerxes' decree to the year Jerusalem's wall and moat were finished in the period of Ezra and Nehemiah. From that time another sixty-two weeks went by until the Messiah was "cut off," a term meaning "executed."

In the early third century, ancient church father Julius Africanus wrote a book entitled, *"On the Weeks and This Prophecy."* Only fragments remain today; but in fragment 16, he tells us how to calculate the exact date by converting the years to days and changing them from the Jewish prophetical calendar to the Roman calendar used in his day. Julius says that the "seventy weeks" prophecy of Daniel 9 started when Artaxerxes gave the decree in his twentieth year. Years later, Sir Robert Anderson recreated the conversion process for our modern calendar as follows: first, the sixty-nine weeks of years ends with the Messiah's death. If we multiply 69 times 7 this gives us the 483 prophetic years between Artaxerxes' decree and the death of the Messiah.

We convert from the Jewish/prophetic calendar to the Gregorian/Roman calendar this way: we take the 483 years times 360 days per year (the sacred Jewish calendar) and that equals 173,880 days. The 173,880 days on the modern calendar comes out to be 476 years and 21 days (476 x 365.25 = 173,859 and 173,880-173,859 = 21). March 14, 444 BC plus 476 years comes out to be March 14, AD 31. We add one year because there was no "0" year between AD and BC. We then add the 21 days. The final date arrives at April 6, AD 32!

70 Weeks Prophecy

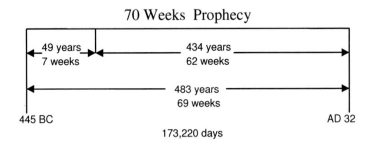

445 BC   AD 32

173,220 days

The prophecy states the Messiah will be cut off, not because He deserved it, but to be a sacrifice for our sins.

The Ancient Rabbis:

When witnessing to Jews, most will say Daniel's 70 weeks prophecy has nothing to do with the Messiah; but the ancient rabbinical writings, including the Talmud, state the prophecy *does* refer to King Messiah. Please point out to them that the Messiah, whoever he was, had to have come before the destruction of the Temple in AD 70. If the Messiah was not Jesus Christ, then who was he? Here is a small list of quotes from the ancient rabbis about this passage in Daniel:

"Daniel has elucidated to us the knowledge of the end times. However, since they are secret, the wise [rabbis] have barred the calculation of the days of Messiah's coming so that the untutored populace will not be led astray when they see that the End Times have already come but there is no sign of the Messiah." *Maimonides: Igeret Teiman, Chapter 3*

"The anointed King is destined to stand up and restore the Davidic Kingdom to its antiquity, to the first sovereignty. He will build the Temple in Jerusalem and gather the strayed ones of Israel together. All laws will return in his days as they were before: Sacrificial offerings are offered and the Sabbatical years and Jubilees are kept, according to all its precepts that are mentioned in the Torah. Whoever does not believe in him, or whoever does not wait for his coming, not only does he defy the other prophets, but also the Torah and Moses our teacher... Bar Kokhba, claimed that he

was King Messiah. He and all the Sages of his generation deemed him King Messiah, until he was killed by sins; only since he was killed, they knew that Bar Kokhba was not the Messiah."
Maimonides: Mishneh Torah, Hilkhot Melakhim Umilchamoteihem, Chapter 11.

"These times (Daniel's 70 Weeks) were over long ago." *Rabbi Judah: Babylonian Talmud, Sanhedrin.*

"I have examined and searched all the Holy Scriptures and have not found the time for the coming of Messiah clearly fixed, except in the words of Gabriel to the prophet Daniel, which are written in the 9th chapter of the prophecy of Daniel." *Rabbi Moses Abraham Levi*

"Similarly, one should not try to calculate the appointed time [for the coming of Messiah]. Our Sages declared: [Sanhedrin 97b] 'May the spirits of those who attempt to calculate the final time [of Messiah's coming] expire!' Rather, one should await [his coming] and believe in the general conception of the matter, as we have explained."
Maimonides: Mishneh Torah, Hilkhot Melakhim Umilchamoteihem, Chapter 12

"...all we need is to do teshuva until Messiah comes, for all the predestined dates for the redemption have already passed."
Talmud: Sanhedrin 97b

"All the time limits for redemption (the coming of Messiah) have passed and the matter now depends only on repentance and good deeds."
Babylonian Talmud: Rabbi Rabh

Notice the rabbis placed a curse on those who would read Daniel 9 and calculate the time of the Messiah's coming to earth. They did this because it clearly points to Jesus Christ.

After the Messiah's Death – The Gap

Sometime after the Messiah's death, a prince would come and destroy the Sanctuary (or Jewish temple) in Jerusalem, Israel. That destruction would result in a Jewish "war," which would bring the complete "desolation" of the county of Israel. This was also directly prophesied in Daniel 11.

"And after threescore and two weeks shall Messiah be cut off, but not for himself: and the people of the prince that shall come shall destroy the city and the sanctuary; and the end thereof *shall be* with a flood, and unto the end of the war desolations are determined." *Daniel 9:26*

These prophecies were fulfilled in this order: Jesus Christ died on the cross in AD 32. Titus destroyed the temple in AD 70. Titus and his father, Vespasian, were Roman generals who besieged the Jerusalem temple. Neither were kings or princes. During the siege, Caesar died and the Roman senate quietly voted Vespasian in as the new emperor and recalled him to Rome. Unknown to Titus, the very day his troops broke though the walls and destroyed the temple, he had become a prince! This fact is another amazing testimony to the accuracy of Bible prophecy.

In AD 71, the Roman officer Turnus Rufus fulfilled Micah's prophecy about plowing over the city of Jerusalem (Micah 3:12). In AD 130 the last Jewish revolt occurred that started the great war. It is known historically as the Bar-Kokhba Rebellion. The rebellion was crushed within two years. In AD 132 the Romans officially desolated the county of Israel. The nation of Israel ceased to exist for 1,816 years until the year AD 1948, when the nation was re-established. In the year 1948 more than ten *other* prophecies were fulfilled as well!

In Daniel chapter 11, the angel gave a complete list of events dating from 536 BC up to AD 1948. Since Daniel predicted the Antichrist would stop the temple sacrifices, there has to be a rebuilt temple. Further, the Jewish people had to return to their homeland, to rebuild it!

These are all events in that gap between the 69th and 70th weeks; but what is the gap for? The gap is for gathering Gentiles for His name. The gap is the church age. James quotes the prophecies of Amos and Isaiah revealing this gap covers the time of the church age.

> "...James answered, saying, Men *and* brethren, hearken unto me: Simeon hath declared how God at the first did visit the Gentiles, to take out of them a people for his name. And to this agree the words of the prophets; as it is written, After this I will return, and will build again the tabernacle of David, which is fallen down; and I will build again the ruins thereof, and I will set it up: That the residue of men might seek after the Lord, and all the Gentiles, upon whom my name is called, saith the Lord, who doeth all these things." *Acts 15:13-17*

What else could this gap be other than the church age? If it is the church age, and the church age ends with the Rapture, then the Rapture has to be pretribulational. We

Events in the Gap	
Messiah dies	32 AD
Temple destroyed	70 AD
Bar-Kokhba War	130 AD
Israel desolated	132 AD
Israel restored	1948 AD
The Rapture	? AD

will see Daniel teaches a pretribulational rapture in chapter 12.

The Seventieth Week

In verse 27 the gap between the sixty-ninth and seventieth weeks ended with the dispersion of the Jews by the Romans. In Daniel 11:33, it ended with the return of the Jews to their land from the Roman expulsion. So the seventieth week must begin sometime after AD 1948.

"²⁷And he shall confirm the covenant with many for one week: and in the midst of the week he shall cause the sacrifice and the oblation to cease, and for the overspreading of abominations he shall make it desolate,ᵖ even until the consummation, and that determined shall be poured upon the desolate."
Daniel 9:27

The Seventieth Week

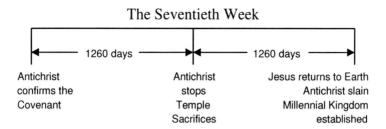

The "he" mentioned here is described exactly the same way by the apostle Paul in 2 Thessalonians 2, where Paul called him the "man of sin" and the "son of perdition." Modern Christians call him the Antichrist.

"³Let no man deceive you by any means: for that day shall not come, except there come a falling away first, and that man of sin be revealed, the son of perdition;" 2 Thessalonians 2:3

Daniel wrote that the last seven years, the seventieth week, would *begin* with the Antichrist enforcing a peace covenant. In the *middle* of the seven-year period, he would stop the sacrifices being performed in the newly

---

ᵖ In Matthew 24:15-16, Jesus stated the Abomination of Desolation mentioned by Daniel would occur right before the Second Coming.

rebuilt temple. At *the end* of the seven-year period the Antichrist would be destroyed by Jesus when He returns to set up His messianic kingdom.

We can also see this same thought taught in Daniel 7 where the "son of man," (Jesus) comes and destroys the "beast," (the Antichrist) and sets up a kingdom that "shall not be destroyed."

Temple Sacrifices and the Sabbath

Daniel wrote that the Antichrist will stop the temple sacrifices, which means they must first be started. Jesus remarked that when the Jews attempt to ..ee when they see the abomination, the Sabbath laws will be in force.

> "[15]When ye therefore shall see the abomination of deso. ition, spoken of by Daniel the prophet, stand in the holy place... pray ye that your flight be not in the winter, neither on the sabbath day:"
> *Matthew 24:15,20*

The two witnesses of Revelation 11:3 will presumably start and continue the temple sacrifices, but the laws regarding the sacrifices and Sabbath laws will have to enforced by the Sanhedrin. The Sanhedrin was a group of seventy-one rabbis that formed the supreme governmental authority for the Jews. They were disbanded in AD 425. In AD 2004, almost 1500 years later, they were reestablished. They are not currently recognized by the official Israeli government but are gaining popularity among the orthodox Jews.

In the near future we will see the power of the Sanhedrin grow, the Sabbath laws reinstituted, and preparations made for temple sacrifices. Then everything will be ready for the two witnesses to appear.

The Peace Covenant
Notice that the Antichrist does not create the points of the peace plan all by himself.

> "[27] And he shall confirm the covenant with many for one week: and in the midst of the week he shall cause the sacrifice and the oblation to cease, and for the overspreading of abominations he shall make *it* desolate, even until the consummation, and that determined shall be poured upon the desolate."
> *Daniel 9:27*

He "confirms" or *ratifies a covenant already in place.* The chart on the next page shows the peace plans proposed between 1947 and 2007. The heart of most peace plans require Israel to trade land for peace. I believe an independent state will be created from the West Bank.

The "many" peoples will include: Israel, Syria, Egypt, possibly the ten nations, and others. Egypt and two other nations will not agree with the peace plan and the Antichrist will attack and conquer them.

The main points of the peace plan will be the reshaping of the Israeli borders, the creation of an independent Palestinian State in the West Bank with full autonomy, and possibly an independent state of Gaza. Daniel 11 predicts after what we call the West Bank becomes an independent state, the Antichrist will create his own international headquarters there.

Date	Peace Agreements	Details
1947	UN Resolution 181	Jerusalem to be an international city, not belonging to Jews
1978	Camp David Accords	Gaza Strip & West Bank become autonomous; Israel withdraws from Sinai
1991	Madrid Conference	Exchange land for peace
1993	Oslo Accords	Withdraw from parts of West Bank & Gaza and allow Palestinians limited self rule
1996	Israel-Jordan treaty	Jordan River water rights and some land went back to Jordan
2000	Camp-David Summit	Israel returns land from the '67 war, Palestinian state in West Bank & Gaza
2007	Annapolis Conference	Independent Palestinian State, Jerusalem to be divided

The Antichrist's Destruction

When some of the ancient church fathers quoted Daniel 9:27, the word "desolate" is replaced with "desolator." With this change in mind, the verse would be saying the Antichrist will confirm a peace agreement with Israel and her surrounding Muslim nations that include an independent Palestinian state in the West Bank. The temple will be rebuilt and temple sacrifices will begin. In the midst of the seventieth week, the Antichrist will stop the temple sacrifices and place the Abomination of Desolation in the temple. He will prosper until the prophecy is fulfilled by the second coming of the Messiah and the Antichrist's destruction.

Ancient Book of Daniel

Daniel
10

In the third year after Cyrus conquered Babylon, 533 BC, God revealed to Daniel even more information about the seven-year Tribulation.

> "¹In the third year of Cyrus king of Persia a thing was revealed unto Daniel, whose name was called Belteshazzar; and the thing *was* true, but the time appointed *was* long: and he understood the thing, and had understanding of the vision." *Daniel 10:1*

The first day of the first month on the Jewish calendar is the festival of Rosh HaShannah, the Jewish New Year. The Festival of Tabernacles occurs on the fifteenth though the twenty-first of the same month. The rituals preformed for the Festival of Tabernacles teach about the messianic kingdom. The twenty-first is HoShanna Rabbah, which instructs us about the end of the messianic kingdom. The twenty-second and twenty-third is the festival called Shimini Azteret, or the eighth conclusion, and the rituals preformed on this date teach about eternity. An angel appeared to Daniel after all these holy days, while the prophecies and symbols were still fresh in his mind.

> "²In those days I Daniel was mourning three full weeks. ³I ate no pleasant bread, neither came flesh nor wine in my mouth, neither did I anoint myself at

all, till three whole weeks were fulfilled. [4]And in the four and twentieth day of the first month, as I was by the side of the great river, which is Hiddekel;[q]" *Daniel 10:2-4*

Even though Daniel was well acquainted with the angels and knew he was greatly loved by them, he still trembled with fear each time he saw them. Their strength and power must be awesome. Each time he saw them, the angels kindly took time with him, to make sure he understood their message.

"[5]Then I lifted up mine eyes, and looked, and behold a certain man clothed in linen, whose loins *were* girded with fine gold of Uphaz: [6]His body also *was* like the beryl, and his face as the appearance of lightning, and his eyes as lamps of fire, and his arms and his feet like in colour to polished brass, and the voice of his words like the voice of a multitude. [7]And I Daniel alone saw the vision: for the men that were with me saw not the vision; but a great quaking fell upon them, so that they fled to hide themselves. [8]Therefore I was left alone, and saw this great vision, and there remained no strength in me: for my comeliness was turned in me into corruption, and I retained no strength. [9]Yet heard I the voice of his words: and when I heard the voice of his words, then was I in a deep sleep on my face, and my face toward the ground. [10]And, behold, an

---

[q] The Hiddekel River is Tigris River.

hand touched me, which set me upon my knees and *upon* the palms of my hands." *Daniel 10:5-10*

Twenty-One Days

Daniel was not the only one who understood the prophecies of God's plan for the Persians to rule until the Greeks would come. Satan and his demonic forces understood, too, and as always, tried to thwart God's plan.

"[11]And he said unto me, O Daniel, a man greatly beloved, understand the words that I speak unto thee, and stand upright: for unto thee am I now sent. And when he had spoken this word unto me, I stood trembling. [12]Then said he unto me, Fear not, Daniel: for from the first day that thou didst set thine heart to understand, and to chasten thyself before thy God, thy words were heard, and I am come for thy words. [13]But the prince of the kingdom of Persia withstood me one and twenty days: but, lo, Michael, one of the chief princes, came to help me; and I remained there with the kings of Persia."
Daniel 10:11-13

In Daniel 10:13, the phrase "and I remained there" can be translated "because I was left there." The Hebrew word for "withstood" can mean either to "prevent by force" or to "be in the way." From Daniel 10:13 and 10:20-11:1 we learn that Gabriel was left to guard the kings of Persia from a demonic threat that would try to depose them and nullify the prophecies, much like Herod tried to thwart the prophecy of a newborn king by killing all babies in Bethlehem.

From the first day Daniel started praying, God ordered Gabriel to go to him and answer some of the questions Daniel was asking about the prophecies. But Gabriel could not leave the kings of Persia unprotected. Gabriel only left when God sent Michael to replace him until he had finished revealing these things to Daniel. God is in control of all things; so why did He allow Gabriel to be delayed for twenty-one days? It was for Daniel's benefit and for ours, as well.

If you pray for complete understanding of prophecy and the ability to witness to others and are still having problems, maybe the problem is not with you, but with Satan, trying his best to prevent you from achieving that goal. Keep praying and studying! Find others of like mind to fellowship with and work with.

The first part of this chapter reveals the twenty-one days were from the third of Tishrei until the twenty-third of Tishrei. Gabriel arrived immediately after the high holy days. These sacred festivals contain rituals that teach about end time prophecy. God allowed Daniel to pray and think about all the symbols of the high holy days before Gabriel came to give him the details. Consult the chapter on *The Fall Festivals* for the prophetic insight these festivals reveal.

End Time Prophecy

From here on though chapter 12 the angel revealed events ranging from 536 BC to AD 1948 and beyond. He told Daniel about the Rapture, the seven-year Tribulation, and the beginning of the millennial reign. Chapters 10 though 12 should be thought of as one long commentary.

"¹⁴Now I am come to make thee understand what shall befall thy people in the latter days: for yet the vision *is* for *many* days." *Daniel 10:14*

Daniel's Fear Calmed

The angel calmed Daniel and began to instruct him about the coming days.

"¹⁵And when he had spoken such words unto me, I set my face toward the ground, and I became dumb. ¹⁶And, behold, *one* like the similitude of the sons of men touched my lips: then I opened my mouth, and spake, and said unto him that stood before me, O my lord, by the vision my sorrows are turned upon me, and I have retained no strength. ¹⁷For how can the servant of this my lord talk with this my lord? for as for me, straightway there remained no strength in me, neither is there breath left in me. ¹⁸Then there came again and touched me *one* like the appearance of a man, and he strengthened me, ¹⁹And said, O man greatly beloved, fear not: peace *be* unto thee, be strong, yea, be strong. And when he had spoken unto me, I was strengthened, and said, Let my lord speak; for thou hast strengthened me." *Daniel 10:15-19*

Prince of Persia

The angel fought against the powers of darkness to make sure the prophecies of the Persian kingdom stood until the Grecian kingdom was ready to take control over Israel.

> "²⁰Then said he, Knowest thou wherefore I come unto thee? and now will I return to fight with the prince of Persia: and when I am gone forth, lo, the prince of Grecia shall come. ²¹But I will shew thee that which is noted in the scripture of truth: and *there* is none that holdeth with me in these things, but Michael your prince." *Daniel 10:20-21*

The angel wanted to elaborate on the "scripture of truth," (verse 21) probably referring to the prophecies of Isaiah about the Medio-Persian coalition under Cyrus conquering the Babylonian Empire. Only Michael and Gabriel fought together against the powers of darkness to make sure the predictions of Scripture came to pass as prophesied.

Daniel
11

The Angel Gabriel began to predict the events from 536 BC to AD 1948. Then he began to talk about the rise of the Antichrist.

Persia (536- 326 BC)
Not only did Gabriel protect Cyrus and Darius, but also encouraged them to free the Jews and rebuild the Jerusalem temple.

> "[1]Also I in the first year of Darius the Mede, *even* I, stood to confirm and to strengthen him. [2]And now will I shew thee the truth. Behold, there shall stand up yet three kings in Persia; and the fourth shall be far richer than *they* all: and by his strength through his riches he shall stir up all against the realm of Grecia." *Daniel 11:1-2*

Darius the Meade ruled from 536 to 530 BC. The four Persian kings were: Cambyses (530-522 BC); Pseudo-Smerdis (522 BC); Darius (522-486 BC); Xerxes I (486-465 BC, See Esther 1:1). Xerxes I, after growing rich, attacked Greece at Sardis of Asia Minor in 480 BC with 60,000 men and 1,200 ships. It was the largest invasion force the world had ever seen up to that time. Still, the Greeks stood their ground and the Persians lost the war.

Greece Under Alexander the Great (326-323 BC)

Alexander the Great was born in Pella in 356 BC. Upon taking the throne of Greece, he began a campaign against the Persian Empire.

> "[3]And a mighty king shall stand up, that shall rule with great dominion, and do according to his will. [4]And when he shall stand up, his kingdom shall be broken, and shall be divided toward the four winds of heaven; and not to his posterity, nor according to his dominion which he ruled: for his kingdom shall be plucked up, even for others beside those."
> *Daniel 11:3-4*

Alexander entered Asia in 334 BC with 34,000 men against Darius' 400,000 men. Even with a much smaller army, within a year he controled Syria. Alexander the Great died at the age of 33, only three years after gaining control of the known world. At the time of his death in 323 BC, none of his children took the throne. Instead, Alexander's kingdom was split into four parts. Each of the four ruling generals of his empire took a portion of the empire for his own. Seleucus Nicator seized Syria, Cassander governed Macedonia (Greece), Lysimachus occupied Thrace (Turkey), and Ptolemy took control of Egypt. There was a fifth general, but he died in a battle just before Alexander did.

Ptolemy I Soter (323-285)

Seleucus Nicator seized control of Syria.

"⁵And the king of the south shall be strong, and *one* of his princes; and he shall be strong above him, and have dominion; his dominion *shall be* a great dominion." *Daniel 11:5*

Then he was deposed and fled to Egypt. He became a general/prince for Ptolemy and recaptured control of Syria. Seleucus ruled Syria from 311-280 BC.

Berenice Marries Antiochus II
Berenice, daughter of Egypt's Pharaoh Ptolemy II, married Antiochus II to form an alliance between Syria and Egypt.

"⁶And in the end of years they shall join themselves together; for the king's daughter of the south shall come to the king of the north to make an agreement: but she shall not retain the power of the arm; neither shall he stand, nor his arm: but she shall be given up, and they that brought her, and he that begat her, and he that strengthened her in *these* times."
Daniel 11:6

Laodice, Antiochus II's first wife, had Berenice and her son executed. She then poisoned Antiochus II and placed her own son, Seleucus II Callinicus, on the throne (246-226 BC).

Ptolemy III Euergetes (246-221 BC)
Berenice's brother, Pharaoh Ptolemy III, attacked the Syrian fortress of Antioch.

"⁷But out of a branch of her roots shall *one* stand up in his estate, which shall come with an army, and shall enter into the fortress of the king of the north, and shall deal against them, and shall prevail: ⁸And shall also carry captives into Egypt their gods, with their princes, *and* with their precious vessels of silver and of gold; *and* he shall continue *more* years than the king of the north. ⁹So the king of the south shall come into *his* kingdom, and shall return into his own land." *Daniel 11:7-9*

Pharaoh Ptolemy III then captured Laodice and put her to death. Berenice's father, Ptolemy II, died about the same time. Ptolemy III recaptured the Syrian & Egyptian gods as spoil, which the Persian king Cambyses had carried off after conquering Egypt in 525 BC.

Seleucus III Ceaunus (226-223 BC) &
Antiochus III the Great (223-187 BC)
Syria's ruler, Seleucus II, had two sons, Seleucus III and Antiochus III.

"¹⁰But his sons shall be stirred up, and shall assemble a multitude of great forces: and *one* shall certainly come, and overflow, and pass through: then shall he return, and be stirred up, *even* to his fortress." *Daniel 11:10*

The two sons started a war with Egypt, but one brother, Seleucus III, died before reaching the battle. Antiochus II pushed all the way to the Egyptian fortress at Raphia in south Israel by 218 BC.

Ptolemy IV Philopator (221-203 BC)
Egypt's Ptolemy IV defeated Antiochus III at Raphia in 217 BC.

> "[11]And the king of the south shall be moved with choler, and shall come forth and fight with him, *even* with the king of the north: and he shall set forth a great multitude; but the multitude shall be given into his hand. [12]*And* when he hath taken away the multitude, his heart shall be lifted up; and he shall cast down *many* ten thousands: but he shall not be strengthened *by* it." *Daniel 11:11-12*

The historian Polybius records over 10,000 soldiers were killed in the battle at Raphia. Ptolemy drove Antiochus III back, but "was not strengthened by it" nor did he conquer Syria. He returned to Egypt.

Ptolemy V Epiphanes (203-181 BC)
Thirteen years after the battle of Raphia, Ptolemy IV died. Antiochus III (the king of the north) then attacked Egypt.

> "[13]For the king of the north shall return, and shall set forth a multitude greater than the former, and shall certainly come after certain years with a great army and with much riches. [14]And in those times there shall many stand up against the king of the south: also the robbers of thy people shall exalt

themselves to establish the vision; but they shall fall. [15]So the king of the north shall come, and cast up a mount, and take the most fenced cities: and the arms of the south shall not withstand, neither his chosen people, neither *shall there be any* strength to withstand." *Daniel 11:13-15*

At this time, a false prophet arose and misled the Jewish people to "establish" his "vision" by supporting the wrong king, Antiochus. The "many" included Philip of Macedon who entered into an agreement to divide Egypt between himself and Antiochus; but the Ptolemic general Scopas crushed the rebellion. Having lost the battle in the south, Antiochus turned back north and captured the port city of Sidon.

Antiochus Controlled Israel
Antiochus was in full control of Israel, the "glorious land," by 197 BC.

"[16]But he that cometh against him shall do according to his own will, and none shall stand before him: and he shall stand in the glorious land, which by his hand shall be consumed."
Daniel 11:16

Antiochus Gave Cleopatra I to Ptolemy V (194 BC)
When Antiochus learned Egypt had made an alliance with Rome, he did not attack Egypt but tried gaining control of Egypt by giving his daughter, Cleopatra, to the 7-yr-old Ptolemy V in marriage.

"¹⁷He shall also set his face to enter with the strength of his whole kingdom, and upright ones with him; thus shall he do: and he shall give him the daughter of women, corrupting her: but she shall not stand *on his side*, neither be for him."
Daniel 11:17

Cleopatra, however, did what was right for Egypt and did not listen to her father.

Roman Consul Defeats Antiochus (190 BC)
Antiochus attacked the coastlands with three hundred ships; but the Roman consul Lucius Cornelius Scipio Asiaticus defeated him at Magnesia, in Asia Minor, in 190 BC.

"¹⁸After this shall he turn his face unto the isles, and shall take many: but a prince for his own behalf shall cause the reproach offered by him to cease; without his own reproach he shall cause *it* to turn upon him. ¹⁹Then he shall turn his face toward the fort of his own land: but he shall stumble and fall, and not be found." *Daniel 11:18-19*

Antiochus died in 187 BC while trying to plunder the temple of Bel, in the province of Elymais.

Seleucus IV Philopator (187-175 BC)
Seleucus IV, son of Antiochus the Great, gave orders to his finance minister to have the Jerusalem temple, the "glory of the kingdom", plundered.

"²⁰Then shall stand up in his estate a raiser of taxes *in* the glory of the kingdom: but within few days he shall be destroyed, neither in anger, nor in battle."
Daniel 11:20

Heliodorus, his finance minister, quickly formed a conspiracy, and within a "few days" Seleucus IV was poisoned.

Antiochus IV Epiphanes (175-164 BC)
Antiochus Epiphanes was most vile. He continually persecuted the Jews until the revolt of the Maccabbees.

"²¹And in his estate shall stand up a vile person, to whom they shall not give the honour of the kingdom: but he shall come in peaceably, and obtain the kingdom by flatteries. ²²And with the arms of a flood shall they be overflown from before him, and shall be broken; yea, also the prince of the covenant. ²³And after the league *made* with him he shall work deceitfully: for he shall come up, and shall become strong with a small people. ²⁴He shall enter peaceably even upon the fattest places of the province; and he shall do *that* which his fathers have not done, nor his fathers' fathers; he shall scatter among them the prey, and spoil, and riches: *yea*, and he shall forecast his devices against the strong holds, even for a time. ²⁵And he shall stir up his power and his courage against the king of the south with a great army; and the king of the south shall be stirred up to battle with a very great and mighty army; but he shall not stand: for they shall forecast devices against him. [26]Yea, they that feed of the portion of his meat shall destroy him, and his army shall overflow: and many shall fall down slain. [27]And both of these kings' hearts *shall be* to do mischief, and they shall speak lies at one table; but it shall not prosper: for yet the end *shall be* at the time appointed." *Daniel 11:21-27*

Antiochus Epiphanes "obtained" the "honor of the kingdom" from his brother Demetrius I, and had Onias III, the "prince of the covenant" assassinated. See *2 Maccabees 4:4-10* below for full details. Antiochus Epiphanes deceived Rome into officially recognizing him. He invaded Israel and most of Egypt. Ptolemy VI Philometer mobilized a large army to stop Antiochus; but his younger brother, Ptolemy VII Physcon, entered into a conspiracy with Antiocus. As a result, Ptolemy VI Philometer was overthrown.

"[4]Onias seeing the danger of this contention, and that Apollonius, as being the governor of Celosyria and Phenice, did rage, and increase Simon's malice, [5]He went to the king, not to be an accuser of his countrymen, but seeking the good of all, both publick and private: [6]For he saw that it was impossible that the state should continue quiet, and Simon leave his folly, unless the king did look thereunto. [7]But after the death of Seleucus, when Antiochus, called Epiphanes, took the kingdom, Jason the brother of Onias laboured underhand to be high priest, [8]Promising unto the king by intercession three hundred and threescore talents of silver, and of another revenue eighty talents: [9]Beside this, he promised to assign an hundred and fifty more, if he might have licence to set him up a place for exercise, and for the training up of youth in the fashions of the heathen, and to write them of Jerusalem by the name of Antiochians. [10]Which when the king had granted, and he had gotten into his hand the rule he forthwith brought his own nation to Greekish fashion."

2 Maccabees 4:4-10 1611 KJV[r]

Antiochus IV Epiphanes Attacked Jerusalem

Antiochus Epiphanes had high priest, Jason, deposed.

"[28]Then shall he return into his land with great riches; and his heart *shall be* against the holy covenant; and he shall do *exploits*, and return to his own land." *Daniel 11:28*

Jason, thinking Antiochus was now powerless, started a rumor that he had died, in hopes of getting the priesthood back. When Antiochus heard all of Israel rejoiced over his supposed death, he attacked with fury. This occurred in 169 BC. See 2 Maccabees 5:5-12 below for details.

"[5]Now when there was gone forth a false rumour, as though Antiochus had been dead, Jason took at the

---

[r] The 1611 KJV contained the Roman Catholic apocrypha and the Anglican Apocrypha but not the Eastern Orthodox Apocrypha.

least a thousand men, and suddenly made an assault upon the city; and they that were upon the walls being put back, and the city at length taken, Menelans fled into the castle: [6]But Jason slew his own citizens without mercy, not considering that to get the day of them of his own nation would be a most unhappy day for him; but thinking they had been his enemies, and not his countrymen, whom he conquered. [7]Howbeit for all this he obtained not the principality, but at the last received shame for the reward of his treason, and fled again into the country of the Ammonites. [8]In the end therefore he had an unhappy return, being accused before Aretas the king of the Arabians, fleeing from city to city, pursued of all men, hated as a forsaker of the laws, and being had in abomination as an open enemy of his country and countrymen, he was cast out into Egypt. [9]Thus he that had driven many out of their country perished in a strange land, retiring to the Lacedemonians, and thinking there to find succour by reason of his kindred: [10]And he that had cast out many unburied had none to mourn for him, nor any solemn funerals at all, nor sepulchre with his fathers. [11]Now when this that was done came to the king's ear, he thought that Judea had revolted: whereupon removing out of Egypt in a furious mind, he took the city by force of arms, [12]And commanded his men of war not to spare such as they met, and to slay such as went up upon the houses." *2 Maccabees 5:5-12 1611 KJV*

Antiochus Attacked Egypt and was Repelled by Rome
Antiochus attacked Egypt again in 168 BC.

> "²⁹At the time appointed he shall return, and come toward the south; but it shall not be as the former, or as the latter. ³⁰For the ships of Chittim shall come against him: therefore he shall be grieved, and return, and have indignation against the holy covenant: so shall he do; he shall even return, and have intelligence with them that forsake the holy covenant." *Daniel 11:29-30*

"Chittim" is the Hebrew word for Rome – see Jasher, Josephus, and the Septuagint. The Roman vessels under the command of Popilius Laenas drove Antiochus back.

Antiochus Typifies the Antichrist (165 BC)
From 158 to 165 BC, Antiochus occupied Jerusalem.

> "³¹And arms shall stand on his part, and they shall pollute the sanctuary of strength, and shall take away the daily *sacrifice*, and they shall place the abomination that maketh desolate." *Daniel 11:31*

Antiochus even sacrificed a pig on the altar in God's holy temple! For three years he controlled Jerusalem. Then Judas Maccabee started a rebellion that drove Syrian forces out of Jerusalem and all of Israel. This event is still commemorated today in the festival of Hanukah.

Daniel prophesies this event almost four hundred years before it was fulfilled by Antiochus Epiphanies. About seventy-five years after Antiochus' death, Jesus referred to this passage in Matthew 24, stating it also refers to the future temple. This is a double-fulfillment prophecy referring to both Antiochus and the future Antichrist.

The Maccabees (164-64 BC)
After Antiochus' three-year occupation, the Maccabees drove him out of Israel.

> "³²And such as do wickedly against the covenant shall he corrupt by flatteries: but the people that do know their God shall be strong, and do *exploits*."
> *Daniel 11:32*

News of the Israelite rebellion crushed his empire. He died a natural death in 164 BC in the city of Tabae. The Macabees then ruled in peace from 164 to 64 BC when the Roman general Pompey conquered Jerusalem.

Roman Occupation and Diaspora (64 BC-AD 1948)
Rome established control of Israel in 64 BC.

> "³³And they that understand among the people shall instruct many: yet they shall fall by the sword, and by flame, by captivity, and by spoil, *many* days."
> *Daniel 11:33*

Rome conquered Israel by the "sword" in 64 BC. The Messiah came and was crucified in AD 32, as we have seen in chapter 9. During this time Jewish Christians converted and instructed many. Rome destroyed the temple by "flame" in AD 70 and then dispersed Israel into either exile or "captivity" among the nations in AD 132. The "many days" turned out to last from AD 132 to AD 1948 – 1816 years!

Rise of the Antichrist

The rest of this vision pertains to the future, after Israel's return in AD 1948.

> "[34]Now when they shall fall, they shall be holpen with a little help: but many shall cleave to them with flatteries. [35]And *some* of them of understanding shall fall, to try them, and to purge, and to make *them* white, *even* to the time of the end: because *it is* yet for a time appointed."
> *Daniel 11:34-35*

Israel continued in exile until the "appointed time" of their return, which was AD 1948. Sometime after 1948, we will see the rise of the Antichrist. The Antichrist will prosper during the whole seven-year Tribulation period. Verse 39 (below) shows he will divide the land of Israel, probably to create a Palestinian state.

Religion of the Antichrist

The religions of the Buddhists, Hindus, and Jews were well known in Daniel's time. Islam is an outgrowth of Jewish and Christian ideas. The Antichrist will not honor a god of the Hindus, Buddhists, Muslims, Jews, or

Christians. Instead he will honor a god of "forces," a god unknown in Daniel's time.

> "[36] And the king shall do according to his will; and he shall exalt himself, and magnify himself above every god, and shall speak marvellous things against the God of gods, and shall prosper till the indignation be accomplished: for that that is determined shall be done. [37] Neither shall he regard the God of his fathers, nor the desire of women, nor regard any god: for he shall magnify himself above all. [38] But in his estate shall he honour the God of forces: and a god whom his fathers knew not shall he honour with gold, and silver, and with precious stones, and pleasant things. [39] Thus shall he do in the most strong holds with a strange god, whom he shall acknowledge *and* increase with glory: and he shall cause them to rule over many, and shall divide the land for gain." *Daniel 11:36-39*

The worship of a god of forces is a very ancient form of paganism that teaches we are evolving into gods. Followers believe the force that once was the original creator God, was emptied out into creation. See *Ancient Paganism* for details. The Antichrist will claim he is the most advanced god.

He will deny Jesus is the only Christ (1 John 2:22), that Jesus is the only son of God (1 John 4:15), that the Christ came in the flesh of Jesus (1 John 4:3), and that Jesus is coming back in the flesh to earth (2 John 7).

The temple will be the strongest of the strongholds until the two witnesses of Revelation are killed. The Antichrist will then place a teraphim (idol) in the temple, according to his religion.

The Great War – Jordan Spared

The Antichrist, while still ruler of Syria, will enforce a peace plan to divide Israel, but allow the temple to be rebuilt. (Perhaps in return for allowing a Palestinian state.) In reaction to this plan, three of the ten nations of his coalition will rebel and move to stop the peace plan.

> "[40]And at the time of the end shall the king of the south push at him: and the king of the north shall come against him like a whirlwind, with chariots, and with horsemen, and with many ships; and he shall enter into the countries, and shall overflow and pass over. [41]He shall enter also into the glorious land, and many *countries* shall be overthrown: but these shall escape out of his hand, *even* Edom, and Moab, and the chief of the children of Ammon."
> *Daniel 11:40-41*

"At the time of the end" refers to the beginning of the seven-year period. The Antichrist will move against Egypt, ruining many countries in the process. The ancient countries of Moab, Ammon, and Edom are now collectively called Jordan. Jordan will not be harmed in this war. Jews that are aware of the predictions in Scripture will flee for safety to Petra, which is in Jordan.

The Three Rebellious Nations

The African nation of Egypt will lead a rebellion to stop the construction of a Jewish temple on the Temple Mount.

"^{42}He shall stretch forth his hand also upon the countries: and the land of Egypt shall not escape. ^{43}But he shall have power over the treasures of gold and of silver, and over all the precious things of Egypt: and the Libyans and the Ethiopians *shall be* at his steps." *Daniel 11:42-43*

"^{4}And the Egyptians will I give over into the hand of a cruel lord; and a fierce king shall rule over them, saith the Lord, the LORD of hosts. ^{5}And the waters shall fail from the sea, and the river shall be wasted and dried up." *Isaiah 19:4-5*

The Antichrist will respond with an attack on Egypt. In Isaiah's description of this battle, all of Egypt is laid waste and the Nile River stops flowing. Daniel adds that Ethiopia and Libya are with Egypt in this war. Now we know who the three rebel nations of Daniel 7:24 are!

The North Eastern War

With Egypt destroyed, another rebellion will begin to arise from the northeast, so the Antichrist will turn his attention there.

"^{44}But tidings out of the east and out of the north shall trouble him: therefore he shall go forth with great fury to destroy, and utterly to make away many." *Daniel 11:44*

Northeast of Egypt is Israel and the West Bank. The Antichrist will return and enforce the peace covenant. He will insist the temple be finished.

The West Bank Kingdom

After the Antichrist squelches the rebellion in Israel and the West Bank, while the temple is being finished, he will select a piece of land for his international headquarters.

> "⁴⁵And he shall plant the tabernacles of his palace between the seas in the glorious holy mountain; yet he shall come to his end, and none shall help him." *Daniel 11:45*

> "⁴⁵He will pitch the tents of his royal pavilion between the seas and the beautiful Holy Mountain; yet he will come to his end, and no one will help him." *Daniel 11:45 NASB*

His headquarters will be in a large city in the area between Mount Moriah (Jerusalem), the Sea of Galilee, and the Mediterranean Sea. This will be in the newly independent Muslim state created in the West Bank. We are not told the name of the city, perhaps because it has not yet been built. The NASB gives a clearer picture of the two seas and Jerusalem. Both versions of Scripture are given for your information.

The Antichrist will finally be destroyed at the Second Coming.

The City of the Antichrist

Some words in the prophecies should not be translated, but read in their original Hebrew. For instance, in Psalm 20:1-3 God sends "help" to teach the people to restore the temple practices. The Hebrew word for help is "Ezra." This is actually a prophecy about God sending a scribe named Ezra to restore the temple practices. The same situation exists in Isaiah 19 where it names the "City of Destruction." See *Ancient Prophecies Revealed* for full details.

This same thing *might* be true here. We know the Antichrist will place his headquarters in a West Bank city, but where? Instead of the Antichrist planting the tents of "his pavilion" Daniel could be saying the Antichrist plants his tents in "אפדנו," the word translated "his pavilion." This word may be pronounced in different ways and may have a completely different meaning in Arabic than it does in Hebrew. To my knowledge there is no such city by that name in the West Bank as of AD 2010. But, perhaps, we should be on the lookout for one in the near future.

Ancient Book of Daniel

Daniel
12

Michael at the Time of the End

Daniel defines the time of the end as the seven-year Tribulation.

> "¹And at that time shall Michael stand up, the great prince which standeth for the children of thy people: and there shall be a time of trouble, such as never was since there was a nation *even* to that same time: and at that time thy people shall be delivered, every one that shall be found written in the book."
> *Daniel 12:1*

The phrase "at that time" refers back to the "time of the end" given in Daniel 11:40. This "time of the end" is the time when the Antichrist is revealed, goes to war with Egypt, persecutes Israel, and then is destroyed at the Second Coming. In other words, it refers to the whole seven-year Tribulation. This is important to realize because some have tried to connect Michael's war with the devil in Revelation 12 with this event. Michael's war with the devil will occur in the *middle* of the seven-year period, not at the beginning. Here, Michael will stand to protect Israel from the Antichrist's wars which occur in the first half of the seven years.

The Rapture

Michael will stand when the "time of trouble" begins. It will begin with an event called "the deliverance" where saints will resurrect out of their graves and ascend to heaven.

> "²And many of them that sleep in the dust of the earth shall awake, some to everlasting life, and some to shame *and* everlasting contempt."
> *Daniel 12:2*

In 1 Thessalonians 4:13-18, Paul wrote the Rapture, or "snatching away" of living believers, will occur at the same time as this resurrection. At the end of the millennial reign the unsaved dead will be resurrected and placed into everlasting contempt.

Increased Understanding of Prophecies

The angel directed Daniel to write down what he knows, as well as the rest of the riddles, because they will be understood by people near the last days.

> "³And they that be wise shall shine as the brightness of the firmament; and they that turn many to righteousness as the stars for ever and ever. ⁴But thou, O Daniel, shut up the words, and seal the book, *even* to the time of the end: many shall run to and fro, and knowledge shall be increased."
> *Daniel 12:3-4*

"Daniel the prophet says 'Shut up the words, and seal the book even to the time of consummation, until many learn, and knowledge be completed. For at that time, when the dispersion shall be accomplished, they shall know all these things.'"
Irenaeus Against Heresies 4.26, AD 170

Ancient church father Irenaeus believed that when the Jews returned to their land ending the Roman diaspora, it would mark the era of the end. So, Bible-believing Christians would begin to completely understand these prophecies after AD 1948. Running "to and fro" probably refers to gathering more information though archeology, like the Dead Sea Scrolls.

Timing of the Rapture and Persecution
Jesus tells us we will not know the day or hour of His coming. But if you find yourself on earth after the Rapture occurs, then you *can* calculate when the Second Coming will be – down to the day!

"[5]Then I Daniel looked, and, behold, there stood other two, the one on this side of the bank of the river, and the other on that side of the bank of the river. [6]And *one* said to the man clothed in linen, which *was* upon the waters of the river, How long *shall it be to* the end of these wonders? [7]And I heard the man clothed in linen, which *was* upon the waters of the river, when he held up his right hand and his left hand unto heaven, and sware by him that liveth for ever that *it shall be* for a time, times, and an half; and when he shall have accomplished to scatter the power of the holy people, all these *things* shall be finished." *Daniel 12:5-7*

Daniel questioned the timing of these events. The angel revealed in verse 7 that there would be three-and-a-half years from the "deliverance," or Rapture, to the beginning of the persecution of the Jews by the Antichrist. The angel did not say when the "people" would be scattered, but when the "power of the people" would be overthrown, which means when the Antichrist invades, sets up the abomination, and starts the persecution, which is the middle of the seven years. We will see that there will be 1,290 days from the middle of the Tribulation until the Second Coming, thus proving a pre-tribulation Rapture!

When is the Second Coming?

Daniel wanted to know exactly when the Messianic kingdom would begin, but the angel refused to reveal that one piece of information to Daniel.

"[8]And I heard, but I understood not: then said I, O my Lord, what *shall be* the end of these *things*? [9]And he said, Go thy way, Daniel: for the words *are* closed up and sealed till the time of the end. [10]Many shall be purified, and made white, and tried; but the wicked shall do wickedly: and none of the wicked shall understand; but the wise shall understand." *Daniel 12:8-10*

Timing of the Abomination and the Second Coming

The angel did reveal that from the Abomination of Desolation (when the Antichrist desecrates the temple by placing a teraphim in it,) until the Second Coming, will be 1,290 days. The angel then cryptically says that those who live long enough to see 1,335 days after the Abomination will be blessed.

> "[11]And from the time *that* the daily *sacrifice* shall be taken away, and the abomination that maketh desolate[s] set up, *there shall be* a thousand two hundred and ninety days. [12]Blessed *is* he that waiteth, and cometh to the thousand three hundred and five and thirty days." *Daniel 12:11-12*

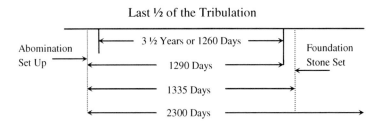

Last ½ of the Tribulation

1260, 1290, 1335, and 2300 Days

In the above chart, we have outlined the last half of the seven-year Tribulation. The first line shows 1,260 days from the Antichrist taking full control and starting the major persecution in the middle of the Tribulation to the Second Coming. The second line of 1,290 days is the

---

[s] In Matthew 24:15-16, Jesus stated the Abomination of Desolation mentioned by Daniel would occur right before the Second Coming.

interval between the setting up of the desolating abomination to the Second Coming. The third line of 1,335 days describes the period from the stopping of the sacrifices and the setting up of the abomination to the cleansing of the Temple Mount and the beginning of the construction of the millennial temple. The fourth line of 2,300 days indicates the days between the abomination to the dedication of the new millennial temple. The 2300 days begins at the same time as the 1290 days. If we subtract 1290 days from 2300 days, we come to 1010 days or another 33 months and 20 days. This means the new Temple will be dedicated two years, nine months and twenty days after the Second Coming.

Daniel's Resurrection

The angel promised Daniel that he would resurrect with the other believers at the beginning of the time of trouble when Michael stands. He will then know all things.

> "¹³But go thou thy way till the end *be*: for thou shalt rest, and stand in thy lot at the end of the days."
> *Daniel 12:13*

Timeline Prophecies

A timeline prophecy is a prediction that when a certain event occurs, then a number of days or years later another event will occur. The best example of this is in Daniel 9:25-26. When the command to rebuild Jerusalem is given, that marks the beginning of 173,220 days which will end with the death of the Messiah.

Death of the Messiah – April 6, AD 32

Let us review how this timeline prophecy was calculated. We convert from the Jewish/prophetic calendar to the Gregorian/Roman calendar this way: we take the 483 years times 360 days per year (the sacred Jewish calendar) and that equals 173,880 days. The 173,880 days on the modern calendar comes out to be 476 years and 21 days (476 x 365.25 = 173,859 and 173,880-173,859 = 21). March 14, 444 BC plus 476 years comes out to be March 14, AD 31. We add one year because there was no "0" year between AD and BC. We then add the 21 days. The final date arrives at April 6, AD 32!

70 Weeks Prophecy

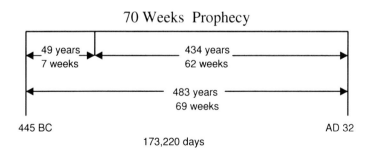

Now anyone can make up a set of rules to make a date end where he wants it to be placed. But, as we will see, when you use the *exact same set of calculations* with three *different* prophecies and they all come out correctly, that cannot be chance or number manipulation.

There are two more timeline prophecies given in the book of Daniel that are very important for modern Christians to know. The first is the date when Israel was designed to be revived, May 14, 1948; and the second, when Israel was predicted to regain control of the Temple Mount, June 7, 1967.

The Second Return – May 14, 1948
Both Daniel and Ezekiel foretold the *exact date* of the reestablishment of Israel.

> "⁴Lie thou also upon thy left side, and lay the iniquity of the house of Israel upon it: according to the number of the days that thou shalt lie upon it thou shalt bear their iniquity. ⁵For I have laid upon thee the years of their iniquity, according to the number of the days, three hundred and ninety days: so shalt thou bear the iniquity of the house of Israel. ⁶And when thou hast accomplished them, lie again on thy right side, and thou shalt bear the iniquity of the house of Judah forty days: I have appointed thee each day for a year." *Ezekiel 4:4-6*

In this passage the sin of Israel and Judah was 390 years and 40 years. To symbolize this, Ezekiel had to lie on his left side for 390 days, a day for each year of Israel's sin, and 40 days on his right side, a day for each year of Judah's sin. The total time then was 430 years of sin. The Babylonian captivity took up 70 years of this punishment, leaving 360 years.

"[14]But if ye will not hearken unto me, and will not do all these commandments; [15]And if ye shall despise my statutes, or if your soul abhor my judgments, so that ye will not do all my commandments, but that ye break my covenant... I will set my face against you, and ye shall be slain before your enemies: they that hate you shall reign over you; and ye shall flee when none pursueth you. [18]And if ye will not yet for all this hearken unto me, then I will punish you seven times more for your sins." *Leviticus 26:14-18*

Here God declares that if Israel does not repent after the Babylonian captivity, when Cyrus freed Israel, then the remaining time would be multiplied sevenfold. If you multiply 360 years by seven, you get 2520 prophetical years. The prophet Daniel predicted this same time period in another way.

In Daniel 4, God punished King Nebuchadnezzar with insanity for seven years, in order to humble him. God had Nebuchadnezzar *act out* a prophecy, just as Ezekiel acted out his 430-day prophecy by lying on his side. In Nebuchadnezzar's case, the restoration of his kingdom after seven years is also a symbolic prophecy that illustrates that the Children of Israel would be restored a second time to *their* land after seven *years* of days. Since the prophetic calendar uses a 360-day year, if you multiply Nebuchadnezzar's seven years by the 360-day calendar, you get 2,520 years – just like Ezekiel's prophecy. From these two prophets we are told the time of the second return of Israel. We will first convert the Jewish years to Roman years the same way we did for the timeline prophecy of the Messiah's death.

Cyrus issued his decree freeing the Jews and declaring the state of Israel to exist again on August 3, 537 BC. Multiply 2,520 Jewish years times 360 days per year to get 907,200 days. The 907,200 days on the modern calendar is 2,483 yrs and 285 days (2,483 yrs x 365.25 = 906,915; 907,200 – 906,915 = 285 days). August 3, 537 BC plus the 2,483 yrs comes to August 3, AD 1946. Add one year because there was no year "0" and the date becomes August 3, AD 1947. When we add the extra 285 days, we arrive at May 14, AD 1948!

This was the very day that the UN declared Israel to be a sovereign state!

Cyrus' Decree   War of Independence

|———————————————————————————————————|

August 3, 537 BC   "907,200 Days"   **May 14, 1948 AD**

Control of the Temple Mount – June 7, 1967
Just as Daniel 4 predicted the reestablishment of the modern state of Israel, Daniel 5 also predicted Israel would take control of the Temple Mount in AD 1967.

In Daniel 5, we read of the account of the handwriting on the wall. This handwriting is an inscription prophecy with a double fulfillment. Daniel left out the first "mene" in this riddle and interpreted only the second Mene, plus the Tekel, and Pharsin as Hebrew *verbs* which literally read "numbered," "weighed," and "divided." Daniel told Belshazzar that the words of the handwriting on that wall meant that he personally had been weighed and found to be godless. Therefore, the days of his kingdom had been numbered and had come to an end. His kingdom would be divided and given to the Medes and Persians.

"^{25}And this is the writing that was written, MENE, MENE, TEKEL, UPHARSIN." *Daniel 5:24*

The double fulfillment is for the latter days. First, notice that mene is stated twice. If we take these words as *nouns* instead of *verbs,* a different meaning

Mene	1,000	garahs
Mene	+1,000	garahs
Tekel	+ 20	garahs
Peres	+ 500	garahs
	2,520	garahs

becomes clear. If we decipher them as nouns, they turn out to be names for weights/money. A mene is 1000 garahs. (A garah is a base unit of weight like our penny.) A tekel is 20 garahs, and a peres is half a mena. "Upharsin" is the Hebrew way of saying "and Peres." So the inscription reads 2,520 garahs or 2,520 periods of time. On this night the control of the temple vessels passed to the children of Israel. Real control of the Temple Mount would be given later by Darius. The actual building of the Temple would be much later still.

This prophecy tells us that from the decree Darius would give granting full control of the Temple Mount, plus 2,520 Jewish years, the children of Israel would again be granted control of the Temple Mount – but not granted the right to build the Temple itself. The calculations for this timeline prophecy are exactly the same as the ones given for 1948. The 2,520 garahs/prophetic years times 360 days comes out to be 907,220 days. The 907,220 days on the modern calendar is 2,483 yrs and 285 days (2,483 yrs x 365.25 = 906915; 907200 – 906915 = 285 days).

Darius's decree to grant the Jews control of the Temple Mount was August 25, 518 BC. This date plus 907,200 days (plus one year changing from BC to AD) brings us to June 7, 1967. *On this exact date* the Israelis again gained control of the Temple Mount during the Six Day War!

Darius Decree   Six Day War

|---|---|

August 25, 518 BC   "907,200 Days"   **June 7, 1967 AD**

The Fall Festivals

In Daniel 9 we learned Daniel was fasting when the angel Gabriel came to reveal the seventy weeks prophecy to him. Jews were commanded to fast on the festival of Yom Kippur, one of the high holy days. In Daniel 10 we learned that God specifically let Daniel pray and fast through the high holy days and did not allow Gabriel to come and reveal more end time prophecy until the high holy days were over. The reason the Holy Spirit identified the time of these events is so we could connect the rituals preformed on these festivals with prophecy.

On Yom Kippur we have the ritual of the scapegoat, which points to the destruction of the Antichrist and the Second Coming. It makes sense, then that at 3:00 PM on Yom Kippur, while Daniel was praying and fasting, Gabriel revealed details about the Tribulation period and the Antichrist's destruction (9:27). Gabriel revealed all the details of prophecy leading up to the time of the Antichrist in chapter 11, only after Daniel fasted and prayed though all of the high holy days.

So that we can understand what Daniel was thinking about, we need to look at the rituals performed on the high holy days.

Outline

The high holy days occur in the month of Tishrei, our September/October. The first and second days of Tishrei are a two-day festival called Rosh HaShannah. This new year festival teaches about the Rapture and Resurrection. The tenth day of Tishrei is the festival of Yom Kippur, which illustrates the Second Coming and Antichrist's destruction. In between are the Days of Awe, or the terrible days, called in Hebrew the Yamin Noraim. They start on the third of Tishrei and finish on the ninth. These seven days symbolize the seven-year Tribulation period.

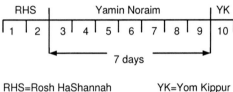

RHS=Rosh HaShannah   YK=Yom Kippur

The First Two Days: Rosh HaShannah - Last Trump

The festival of Trumpets is known by several names. Rosh HaShannah, meaning the "head of the year," or New Year's Day, is one name. It is also called Yom ha-Din, Day of Judgment, and Yom ha-Zikkaron, the Day of Remembrance, by the ancient rabbis. Still another name for this festival is Yom Turah, meaning the "day of the awakening blast." This name is taken from Leviticus 23:24.

"Speak unto the children of Israel, saying, In the seventh month, in the first *day* of the month, shall ye have a sabbath, a memorial of blowing of trumpets, an holy convocation." *Leviticus 23:24*

The Hebrew word translated here as "blowing of trumpets" is the Hebrew word "turah." It is normally used to refer to a trumpet blast that awakens troops. The ancient rabbis taught this prophetically referred to the time of the Resurrection.

"The resurrection of the dead will occur on Yom haDin, which is also called Rosh haShannah," *Talmud, Rosh haShannah 16b*

"It has been taught: Rabbi Eliezer says, 'In the month of Tishri the world was created, ...and in Tishrei they will be redeemed in the time to come.'" *Talmud, Rosh haShannah 10b-11a*

Rabbi Herman Kieval wrote *The High Holy Days,* which was first published in 1959. In his work he states that many Jewish scholars, including Theodore Gaster, have taught that the festival of Rosh haShannah was called the festival of the Last Trump from ancient times.

In an ancient Jewish midrash called *Prike deR' Eliezer* the origin of these terms is explained. The left horn of the ram sacrificed by Abraham in place of Isaac, is called the First Trump, and was blown on Mount Sinai. Its right horn, called the Last Trump, will be blown to herald the coming of the Messiah.

Notice in 1 Corinthians, Paul uses festival language a number of times. In 1 Corinthians 5:6-7 he calls Jesus our Passover lamb, and in 1 Corinthians 5:8 we keep the feast with unleavened bread. All through chapters 11-14 Jesus is connected with the Feast of Weeks and in 1 Corinthians 15:20-23 Jesus is our First Fruits. So when Paul states the Rapture will occur at the Last Trump, it should be clear he is referring to the *festival* of the Last Trump, or Rosh haShannah.

> "Behold, I shew you a mystery; we shall not all sleep, but we shall all be changed, in a moment, in the twinkling of an eye, at the last trump: for the trumpet shall sound, and the dead shall be raised incorruptible, and we shall be changed."
> *1 Corinthians 15:51-52*

Paul does not necessarily mean that the Rapture will occur during the two days of Rosh haShannah, but that the rituals preformed on Rosh haShannah prophetically teach about the Rapture.

Part of the ritual for Rosh haShannah consists of the "Zikhronot," or Book of Remembrance being opened and the "Natzal" occurs. Natzal is the Hebrew word that corresponds to the Greek word "harpizo." Harpizo is the New Testament Greek word we translate as "Rapture," which means to snatch away suddenly by force.

In discussing the Rapture in 1 Thessalonians 4 and 5, Paul wrote that of the "times and seasons" you should not be ignorant. He means we should know about the seven festivals that prophetically teach about the coming of our Lord.

Why the "last trump" is not the seventh trump.

Many Christians who are ignorant of the seven festivals *assume* that the "last trump" Paul talked about in 1 Corinthians 15:52-53 is the same as the seventh trumpet recorded in Revelation 11:15. One major problem with this point of view is that Paul wrote 1 Corinthians before his death in AD 67. John wrote the book of Revelation in AD 95. Paul could not be quoting a book written more than twenty-five years after his death! Knowing this, let us go on and see what we can learn about the seven-year Tribulation period from these festivals.

Day of Concealment

Another term for Rosh haShannah is Yom haKeseh. Yom haKeseh means "the Day of Concealment." The term was taken from Psalm 81:3 by the ancient rabbis.

> "Blow up the trumpet in the new moon, in the time appointed, on our solemn feast day." *Psalm 81:3*

The Hebrew word "keseh" is translated "new moon" in this passage. A new moon is said to be concealed, as opposed to a full moon which is revealed. This is yet another picture of the concealment of the church by the Rapture.

The Next Seven Days: Days of Awe

The chart on the next page shows the outline of this time period with the fall festivals. The New Year starts with Rosh HaShannah (RHS). Remember, this is a two-day festival occurring on the first and second of Tishrei.

> "From the time of R. Johanan b. Zakkai; Palestine, like other countries, observed Rosh ha-Shannah for two days. The Zohar lays stress on the universal observance of two days."
> *Jewishencyclopedia.com; New-Year*

The tenth of Tishrei marks the festival of Yom Kippur (YK), also known as the "Day of Atonement." The ritual preformed on Yom Kippur teaches about the destruction of the Antichrist and the Second Coming of the Messiah.

The seven days between Rosh HaShannah and Yom Kippur are called the Yomin Noraim, which means the "days of awe" or the terrible days. The ancient rabbis took this name from Joel 2:11, which refers to the Day of the Lord.

> " [11]And the LORD shall utter his voice before his army: for his camp is very great: for he is strong that executeth his word: for the day of the LORD is great and very terrible [Nora]; and who can abide it?" *Joel 2:11*

Notice, the Yomin Noraim are the seven days/years that occur between the Rapture/Resurrection and the Second

Coming! This gives a perfect picture of the pretribulational Rapture of the church.

"and to wait for His Son from heaven, whom He raised from the dead, that is Jesus, who **rescues** [author's emphasis] us from the wrath to come."
1 Thessalonians 1:10 NASB

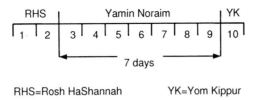

RHS=Rosh HaShannah   YK=Yom Kippur

The Tenth Day: Day of Atonement - Great Trump

The Festival of Trumpets is called the Festival of "The Awakening Blast" and the "Last Trump." In contrast with this, the festival of the Day of Atonement is called the Festival of the "Great Trump."

This helps us organize the prophecies in Scripture. Whenever we see "last trump" in Scripture, we know it is referring to the time of the Rapture/Resurrection of believers. Whenever we see the "great trump" we know it is referring to the Second Coming. To verify the different festival names; look them up in the Encyclopedia Judaica.

During the festival of Yom Kippur there was a prophetic ceremony that involved two goats. Two nearly identical goats were selected and brought before the high priest.

The high priest placed his hands randomly on one of the goats. Another priest brought out the Qalephi, a box containing two lots. The high priest withdrew one of the

Newly created lots for the Yom Kippur ceremony

lots and placed it with the first goat. Then the high priest withdrew the other lot for the second goat. On one lot was engraved לאדני, meaning "for the Lord." The goat that randomly acquired the lot "for the Lord" was sacrificed for the sins of the people. This animal was a perfect representation of the Messiah dying for the sins of the world. The other lot was engraved with לעזאזל, which meant "for Azazel." This has commonly been translated "scapegoat," but Azazel actually was a proper name. Moses wrote about this ceremony in Leviticus 16 saying:

> "Aaron shall cast lots for the two goats, one lot for the LORD and the other lot for the scapegoat [Azazel]. Then Aaron shall offer the goat on which the lot for the LORD fell, and make it a sin offering. But the goat on which the lot for the scapegoat fell shall be presented alive before the LORD, to make atonement upon it, to send it into the wilderness as the scapegoat [to Azazel]." *Leviticus 16:8-10 NASB*

The Mishnah is a book written about AD 200. It contains the oral Torah, with the exact details explaining how to perform the rituals described the Old Testament. In Yoma

4.2 of the Mishnah, details are given concerning the ceremony of the two goats.

A scarlet-colored wool cord was specially created for this ceremony. One piece of this cord was tied to one of the horns of the Azazel goat. Another piece of the cord was tied around the neck of the Lord's goat.

Leviticus describes the Azazel goat being sent into the "wilderness." But the Mishnah gives greater detail about that part of the ritual in Yoma 6. The two goats were required to be alike in appearance, size, and weight. The "wilderness" that the Azazel goat was taken to was actually a ravine. Between Jerusalem and this ravine were ten stations or booths. Since it was a High Holy Day, it was forbidden to travel very far. One priest took the Azazel goat from Jerusalem to the first booth. Then another priest took it from the second to the third booth. This continued until a priest took it from the tenth booth to the ravine. In ancient times this ravine was called Bet HaDudo. Its whereabouts is currently unknown. The Mishnah then explains how the priest took the crimson cord off the goat, cut it into two pieces, and tied one piece to the large rock on the cliff of the ravine, and the other piece to the horns of the goat. He then pushed the goat off the cliff! Before it would be halfway down the cliff, it was already torn into pieces.

If the ritual was properly done, the crimson cord would turn snow white. At that point the priest would signal the tenth booth, which would in turn signal the ninth, all the way back to the first booth, which would signal the high priest standing at the door of the sanctuary. When the high priest learned the crimson thread had turned white, he finished the ritual by quoting Isaiah 1:18.

> "'Come now, and let us reason together,' says the LORD, 'though your sins are as scarlet, they will be as white as snow; though they are red like crimson, they will be like wool.'" *Isaiah 1:18 NASB*

The Meaning of the Ritual

It has been speculated that the scapegoat represents Jesus taking away our sin. That is one possible interpretation. If the information given in the Mishnah is correct, another picture emerges. Two identical goats, one dedicated to God, the other dedicated to Satan. One goat represents the Messiah and the other represents the Antichrist. The ravine represents, and probably is located in, the valley of Megiddo. The only way to tell the difference between the Messiah and the Antichrist is to know the Lord's will by carefully studying the Word of God. At the Second Coming, the Antichrist will be destroyed in Megiddo, in a battle called Armageddon.

Appendix A
Ancient Church Commentary

The disciples of the apostles taught premillennialism, which means they taught that Jesus will return to earth in the future and set up a kingdom that will last for a literal one thousand years as prophesied in Scripture. He will reign from the city of Jerusalem. Prior to this, the Jews were to return and reestablish the state of Israel (which occurred in AD 1948). Then the Antichrist would rise and the Jerusalem temple would be rebuilt during the seven years right before the Second Coming.

In the years AD 200-300, a movement arose teaching these doctrines were symbolic of historical events. We will see that after an event in church history called the *Schism of Nepos*, the whole church abandoned the teachings of the twelve apostles and adopted what is now called Amillennialism.

Some ancient church fathers taught the second coming of Jesus would occur at the end of six thousand years of human history. Here is what the early church fathers said about the end times:

1. There will be a literal one-thousand-year reign of Christ.
2. There will be a literal Antichrist and a tribulation period lasting seven years.

3. The Jews will return to their land and rebuild their temple in Jerusalem.

First, let us look at what the ancient church fathers said about the thousand-year reign of Jesus Christ on earth.

Papias *AD 70-155*

Fragment 6 – After the resurrection of the dead, Jesus will personally reign for one thousand years. I was taught this by the apostle John, himself.

Tertullian AD 190-210

Against Marcion 3.25 – The millennial reign, resurrection, and the new Jerusalem are literal.

Irenaeus AD 178

Against Heresies 5.35 – The Resurrection of the Just takes place after the destruction of the Antichrist and all nations under his rule. Many believers will make it through the Tribulation and replenish the earth. In the Resurrection we will have fellowship and communion with the holy angels, and union with spiritual beings. The new heavens and earth will be created, and then the new Jerusalem will descend. These are all literal things, and Christians who allegorize them are immature.

Notice Irenaeus' last quote. Christians who are Amillennialists or Postmillennialists may be true

Christians; but they are very immature in their faith. If they cannot understand something so simple as the return of Jesus, what else have they mixed up in their faith?

The Six Thousand Years

The idea that Jesus will return to set up His millennial kingdom in the Jewish year 6,000 is taught by several ancient church fathers. The First Coming of Jesus Christ was about 4,000 years after Creation. These ancient church fathers taught the Second Coming would be about AD 2000. The most descriptive is in the Epistle of Barnabas which devotes an entire chapter on this issue. Remember, *this does not mean they were correct*; but if they believed and taught this, it proves the ancient Christians were Premillennial. Here are a few quotes on the issue. With the calendars being confused and inaccurate, we cannot say for certain when the year 6,000 will occur. An approximate range would be between the years AD 2030 and 2067, although it could occur even earlier. See *Ancient Post-Flood History* for more information on the historical timeline.

Barnabas, AD 100

Epistle of Barnabas 15:7-9 – Therefore, children, in six days, or in six thousand years, all the prophecies will be fulfilled. Then it says, He rested on the seventh day. This signifies at the Second Coming of our Lord Jesus, He will destroy the Antichrist, judge the ungodly, and change the sun, moon, and stars. Then He will truly rest during the Millennial Reign, which is the seventh day.

Irenaeus, AD 180

Against Heresies 5.28 – The day of the Lord is as a thousand years; and in six days created things were completed. It is evident, therefore, they will come to an end in the six thousandth year.

Hippolytus, AD 205

Fragment 2; Commentary on Daniel 2.4 – The Sabbath is a type of the future kingdom... for "a day with the Lord is as a thousand years." Since, then, in six days the Lord created all things, it follows that in six thousand years all will be fulfilled.

Commodianus, AD 240

Against the Gods of the Heathens 35 – We will be immortal when the six thousand years are completed.

Against the Gods of the Heathens 80 – Resurrection of the body will be when six thousand years are completed, and after the one thousand years [millennial reign], the world will come to an end.

Victorinus, AD 240

Commentary on Revelation 20.1-3 – Satan will be bound until the thousand years are finished. That is, after the sixth day.

Methodius, AD 290

> *Ten Virgins 9.1* – In the seventh millennium we will be immortal and truly celebrate the Feast of Tabernacles.

Lactantius, AD 304

> *Divine Institutes 7.14* – The sixth thousandth year is not yet complete. When this number is complete, the consummation must take place.

In the first three centuries, the church fathers taught the following were still future events and would take place in this order:

1. The Roman Empire would fall apart. (This took place in AD 476.)
2. Out of what was the Roman Empire, ten nations would spring up. These are the ten toes and ten horns of Daniel's prophecy. (This is still future.)
3. A literal man, possessed by a demon, called the Antichrist, will ascend to power. (This is still future.)
4. The Antichrist's name, if spelled out in Greek, will add up to the number 666.
5. The Antichrist will sign a peace treaty between the Jews in Israel and the local non-believers there. This treaty will be for a seven-year period.
6. This seven years' treaty is the last seven years of the "sets of sevens" prophecy in Daniel 9.
7. At the end of the seven years, Jesus will return to earth, destroy the Antichrist, and establish a literal reign of peace that will last for one thousand years.

The ancient church fathers state they were taught these things by the apostles, and were also told that anyone who rises up in the church and begins to say any of these things are symbolic, are immature Christians who cannot rightly divide the word of God, and should not be heard. (Today this includes most of, but not all of, the Reformed, Presbyterian, Lutheran, Eastern Orthodox, and Roman Catholic churches).

Here are some of the quotes and references from the early church fathers on the End Times:

Justin Martyr AD 110-165

> *Dialogue 32* – The Man of Sin, spoken of by Daniel, will rule two [three] times and a half, before the Second Advent.

> *Dialogue 81* – There will be a literal one-thousand-year reign of Christ.

> *Dialogue 110* – The man of apostasy, who speaks strange things against the Most High, shall venture to do unlawful deeds on the earth against the believers.

Irenaeus AD 178

> *Against Heresies 5.25* – In 2 Thessalonians, the "falling away" is an apostasy and there will be a literal rebuilt temple. In Matthew 24, the "abomination spoken by Daniel" is the Antichrist sitting in the temple as if he were Christ. The abomination will start in the middle of Daniel's 70th week and last for a literal three years and six months. The little horn [11th] is the Antichrist.

Against Heresies 5.26 – The Roman Empire will first be divided and then be dissolved. Ten kings will arise from what used to be the Roman Empire. The Antichrist slays three of the kings and is then the eighth king among them. The kings will destroy Babylon, then give the Babylonian kingdom to the Beast and put the church to flight. After that, the kings will be destroyed by the coming of the Lord. Daniel's horns are the same as the ten toes. The clay and iron mixture of the ten toes represents the fact that some kings will be active and strong, while others will be weak and ineffective. It also means the kings will not agree with each other.

Against Heresies 5.30 – The name of the Antichrist equals 666 if spelled out in Greek. Do not even try to find out the number of the name until the ten kings arise. The Antichrist shall come from the tribe of Dan. That is why the tribe of Dan is not mentioned in the Apocalypse. The fourth kingdom seen by Daniel is Rome. Titan is one Greek word that totals 666. [Each letter in Greek also represents a number, so every Greek word also totals a number.] The rebuilt temple will be in Jerusalem.

Against Heresies 5.35 – The Resurrection of the Just takes place after the destruction of the Antichrist and all nations under his rule. Many believers will make it through the Tribulation and replenish the earth. In the Resurrection we will have fellowship and communion with the holy angels, and union with spiritual beings. The new heavens and earth are first created and then the new Jerusalem descends. These are all literal things, and Christians who allegorize them are immature Christians.

Tertullian AD 190-210

Against Marcion 3.5 – There will be a literal one-thousand-year reign of Jesus Christ.

Against Marcion 3.25 – Millennial reign, resurrection, and the New Jerusalem are literal.

Against Marcion 5.16 – The Antichrist will be a real man and sit in a real temple.

Treatise of the Soul 1.50 – Enoch and Elias will come back to die. They are the two witnesses of Revelation.

Origen AD 230

Against Celsus 2:49 – Quotes Paul, saying the Antichrist is a literal person who works false miracles.

Against Celsus 6:45 – There is a literal future Antichrist coming.

Against Celsus 6:46 – The prophecies in Daniel and 1 Thessalonians are real prophesies about the end of the world. There will be a literal rebuilt temple.

Commodianus AD 240

Against the Gods of the Heathens 35 – Resurrection is at the end of the six thousand years [since Creation].

Against the Gods of the Heathens 41 – Isaiah said: This is the man [the Antichrist] who moves the world against so many kings, and under whom the land shall become desert. Hear ye how the prophet foretold... the whole earth on all sides, for seven years shall tremble.

Against the Gods of the Heathens 44 –Those who were not martyred under the Antichrist will marry and have children during the one thousand years. There will be no rains, snow, or cold during the one thousand years.

Against the Gods of the Heathens 80 – Resurrection of the body will be when six thousand years are completed, and after another one thousand years the world has come to an end.

Lactantius AD 285

Divine Institutes 7:14 – There will be a total of six thousand years until the millennium.

Divine Institutes 7:25 – The end of days is after the fall of Rome at the end of six thousand years. Even your Sibylline oracles teach this.

Epitome of Divine Institutes 72 – The righteous will be raised unto eternal life... But when the thousand years shall be fulfilled... the wicked will be raised for judgment.

Schism of Nepos

If Premillennialism was so clearly taught, complete with eyewitness testimony and warnings that wolves would arise in the church and change these teachings, then how did the change take place?

Since the one thousand years is mentioned only in the book of Revelation, the focus is on how Revelation should properly be interpreted. Most of the older denominations do not believe it should be interpreted as literal, or, at least, they never talk about it. The Eastern Orthodox Church, for instance, teaches that the book of Revelation was added to the canon of Scripture only on the condition that it would never be read in a public service. This supposedly happened just prior to the Council of Constantinople in 381. This is the same council that supposedly condemned Pre-millennialism. The problem with this belief is that the "Tome and Anathemas," written from the decisions of this council, no longer exists. So no one really knows what took place during this Council of Constantinople.

About two hundred years earlier, in AD 170, a document was written detailing what should be included in the New Testament Canon and why. This document is called the Muratorian Canon Fragment, because only a portion of it still exists. It clearly states "We receive the Apocalypses of John and Peter only. Some of us do not wish the Apocalypse of Peter to be read in church." We can see from very early times the book of Revelation was accepted and read in church. Either the Orthodox legend is a complete myth or it is mixed up with the statement that some did not like the spurious "Apocalypse of Peter" to be read in church. In either case, the book of the Revelation, written by John, has always been accepted and taken very literally.

Eusebius wrote his *Ecclesiastical History*" in AD 325. In *Ecclesiastical History 3.39* he records Papias' testimony that the apostle John taught him that Jesus would literally come back in the flesh and reign for one thousand years.

The apostle John had many enemies. But his arch-rival was the Gnostic, Cerinthus. In Eusebius's *Ecclesiastical History 7.24-25* we learn that in the apostle John's time, when everyone still believed in the literal interpretation of the Book of Revelation, Cerinthus added the teaching that the Millennium would be for the gratifying of the sensual appetites, like food, drink, and sex. (One can see where the Muslims get the idea that martyrs go to a paradise with all the food and wine they want and their seventy-two virgins!)

Most Christians simply ignored the ravings of Cerinthus the Gnostic; but these perverse teachings led some early Christians to reject the book of Revelation; or to accept it, but view the thousand years as symbolic. When the allegorical interpretation started really gaining ground about AD 290, an Egyptian bishop named Nepos wrote a book entitled *Refutation of the Allegorists*. This book no longer exists, but Eusebius states it had many of the quotes of the fathers we have given above, plus a lot of history about the Gnostics. The movement for Amillennialism used his *"Refutation"* to convince many he was secretly trying to revive the heretical teaching of Cerinthus. This caused even more Christians to switch to the Amillennial view, and most of the remaining Christians to avoid the issue all together.

By the fourth century, Amillennialism was the standard; and the legend that the book of Revelation was never originally designed to be read or studied by the average Christian, was firmly in place.

Nepos and the Millennium are also mentioned by Dionysius in his *Promises 1.1*. Victorinus' *Commentary on Revelation* also mentions Cerinthus in chapter 22.

It is an interesting to note that Eusebius, in AD 325, takes the Amillennial position. He may have had to "officially" accept the party line in order to write his church history, but buried deep within his history is the complete story of how it happened.

Appendix B
Tribulation Outline

This outline is adapted from the book *Ancient Prophecies Revealed*, which lists over 500 Bible prophecies in the order of fulfillment. This list only covers the seven-year Tribulation period, referencing prophecies 387 to 468. There are eighty-two prophecies in all, ranging from the Rapture to the Second Coming.

Prophecies the Tribulation	References
387. Apostasy comes	2 Thess. 2:6-7
388. Restrainer leaves	2 Thess. 2:6-7
389. Antichrist revealed when he ratifies the peace covenant	Dan. 9:27; 2 Thess. 2:3
390. The Tribulation (Daniel's 70th week) will begin a seven-year period with a signed peace covenant	Dan. 9:27
391. New Jerusalem Temple built	2 Thess. 2:4; Dan. 9:27
392. Temple Mount divided	Ezek. 43; Rev. 12
393. Gospel preached to all nations	Matt. 24:14
394. Elijah returns and preaches against the Antichrist for 3.5 years	Mal. 4:5-6

The Antichrist's rise to power

395. He will be revealed when the ten nations are in power	Dan. 7:24
396. He will be different from the ten kings	Dan. 7:24
397. He will rise to power by trickery	Dan. 11:21-24
398. He will give great honor to those who acknowledge him and cause them to rule over many, and will parcel out land for a price	Dan. 11:39

The Antichrist's identifying characteristics

399. The letters of his name will equal 666 in Greek	Rev. 13:16-17
400. Antichrist's right eye and one arm damaged	Zech. 11:17

The wars fought by the Antichrist in his rise to power

401. He will subdue three kings (of the ten) then ten kings will be given into his hand for 42 months	Dan. 7:8,24,25
402. Egypt, the King of the South, will attack the Antichrist	Dan. 11:40
403. Egypt and many other countries will fall to him.	Dan. 11:42
404. Syria, the King of the North, will attack the Antichrist	Dan. 11:40
405. Many other nations will be destroyed by the Antichrist	Dan. 11:40
406. He will destroy to an extraordinary degree	Dan. 8:24
407. He will destroy many while they are at ease (at peace)	Dan. 8:25
408. The Libyans and Ethiopians will follow at his heels	Dan. 11:43
409. Rumors from the east and north will disturb him and he will annihilate many	Dan. 11:44
410. One-fourth of the world's population will be destroyed under his "leadership"	Rev. 6:8
411. Animals will attack	Amos 5:18; Rev. 6:8

Antichrist rules supreme

412. The remaining seven nations will willingly accept his leadership	Rev. 17:12-13
413. He will pitch the tent of his royal pavilion between the seas and the holy mountain.	Dan. 11:45

The Person of the Antichrist

414. He will be a man and the king/ruler of a nation	Dan. 8:23
415. He will be insolent and skilled in intrigue	Dan. 8:23
416. His power will be mighty, but not by his own power (demonic power)	Dan. 8:24
417. He will prosper and perform his will	Dan. 8:24
418. Through shrewdness, he will cause deceit to succeed	Dan. 8:25
419. He will magnify himself in his heart	Dan. 8:25
420. He will do as he pleases	Dan. 11:36
421. He will fling truth to the ground and perform his will and prosper	Dan. 8:12

The Religion of the Antichrist

422. He will speak out against the Most High	Dan. 7:25
423. He will intend to make alterations to the times and laws	Dan. 7:25
424. He will exalt himself above every known god	Dan. 11:36; 2 Thess. 2:4

425. He will speak monstrous things against the God of gods — Dan. 11:36

426. He will show no regard for the god of his fathers — Dan. 11:37

427. He will worship a strange god that his ancestors never knew — Dan. 11:38

428. He will honor a strange god of forces — Dan. 11:38

429. He will not regard the desire of women — Dan. 11:37

430. He will magnify himself to be equal with the Commander of the Host (Jesus) — Dan. 8:11

431. He will oppose the Prince of princes — Dan. 8:25

432. He will deny the Father and Son — 1 John 2:22

433. He will deny Jesus is the Son of God — 1 John 4:15

434. He will deny Jesus is *the* Christ — 1 John 2:22

435. He will deny Jesus came in the flesh — 1 John 4:3

436. He will deny Jesus will come back in the flesh — 2 John 7

The Invasion of Israel

437. He will take action against the strongest of fortresses with the help of a foreign god (the strange god) — Dan. 11:39

438. Armies surround Jerusalem — Luke 21:20

439. The Jewish people will be expelled from their half of Jerusalem — Zech. 14:2

440. Antichrist's kingdom grows exceedingly great toward the south, east, and toward Israel — Dan. 8:9

441. He will destroy mighty men and the holy people — Dan. 8:24

442. He will enter the beautiful land and many countries will fall — Dan. 11:41

443. Jordan will escape out of his hand — Dan. 11:41

The Abomination of Desolation

444. He will take his seat in the temple of God, displaying himself as God — 2 Thess. 2:4

445. He will oppose and exalt himself above every so-called god or object of worship — 2 Thess. 2:4

446. God will send upon non-Christians a deluding influence so that they will believe *the* lie — 2 Thess. 2:11

447. Antichrist will place a teraphim in the new temple — Rev. 13:14-18

448. He will grow in power and will cause some of the host to fall — Dan. 8:10

449. The place of God's sanctuary will be thrown down — Dan. 8:11

450. He will remove the regular sacrifice from God — Dan. 8:11

451. On account of transgression, the host (idol or army) will be given over to the horn, along with the regular sacrifice — Dan. 8:12

452. Peace covenant will be broken	Zech; Dan; 2 Thess. 2
453. The 2300 days will start	Dan. 8:13-14
454. The 1290 days will start	Dan. 12:11-12
455. The 1335 days will start	Dan. 12:11-12

The Persecution

456. He will wage war with the saints and overpower them	Dan. 7:21
457. He will wear down the saints of the Highest One	Dan. 7:25
458. The saints of the Highest One will be given into his hands for a time, times, and half a time	Dan. 7:25
459. Antichrist will persecute Messianic Jews	Rev. 12:17
460. 1260 days will start	Dan. 12:6-7
461. Some of the Jews will flee to Petra/Bozrah	Rev. 12:6

The Wrath

462. The sign of the sun and moon going dark will occur	Joel 2:30-32; Rev. 6:12-17
463. The wrath of God will begin	Rev. 6:16-17
464. Days will be shortened	Matt. 24:22
465. The wrath of God will end	Rev. 15:1

The Antichrist's Destruction

466. He will be broken without human agency (by Christ)	Dan. 8:25
467. He will prosper until the indignation is finished (until the Second Coming)	Dan. 11:36
468. He will be destroyed and thrown into the fire	Dan. 7:11; 2 Thess. 2

Other Books by
Ken Johnson, Th.D.

Ancient Post-Flood History
Historical Documents That Point to a Biblical Creation.

This book is a Christian timeline of ancient post-Flood history based on Bible chronology, the early church fathers, and ancient Jewish and secular history. This can be used as a companion guide in the study of Creation Science.

Some questions answered: Who were the Pharaohs in the times of Joseph and Moses? When did the famine of Joseph occur? What Egyptian documents mention these? When did the Exodus take place? When did the Kings of Egypt start being called "Pharaoh" and why?

Who was the first king of a united Italy? Who was Zeus and where is he buried? Where did Shem and Ham rule and where are they buried?

How large was Nimrod's invasion force that set up the Babylonian Empire, and when did this invasion occur? What is Nimrod's name in Persian documents?

How can we use this information to witness to unbelievers?

Ancient Seder Olam
A Christian Translation of the 2000-year-old Scroll

This 2000-year-old scroll reveals the chronology from Creation through Cyrus' decree that freed the Jews in 536 BC. The *Ancient Seder Olam* uses biblical prophecy to prove its calculations of the timeline. We have used this technique to continue the timeline all the way to the reestablishment of the nation of Israel in AD 1948.

Ancient Book of Daniel

Using the Bible and rabbinical tradition, this book shows that the ancient Jews awaited King Messiah to fulfill the prophecy spoken of in Daniel, Chapter 9. The Seder answers many questions about the chronology of the books of Kings and Chronicles. It talks about the coming of Elijah, King Messiah's reign, and the battle of Gog and Magog.

This scroll and the Jasher scroll are the two main sources used in Ken's first book, *Ancient Post-Flood History*.

Ancient Prophecies Revealed
500 Prophecies Listed In Order Of When They Were Fulfilled

This book details over 500 biblical prophecies in the order they were fulfilled; these include pre-flood times though the First Coming of Jesus and into the Middle Ages. The heart of this book is the 53 prophecies fulfilled between 1948 and 2008. The last 11 prophecies between 2008 and the Tribulation are also given. All these are documented and interpreted from the Ancient Church Fathers.

The Ancient Church Fathers, including disciples of the 12 apostles, were firmly premillennial, pretribulational, and very pro-Israel.

Ancient Book of Jasher
Referenced in Joshua 10:13; 2 Samuel 1:18; 2 Timothy 3:8

There are 13 ancient history books mentioned and recommended by the Bible. The Ancient Book of Jasher is the only one of the 13 that still exists. It is referenced in Joshua 10:13; 2 Samuel 1:18; and 2 Timothy 3:8. This volume contains the entire 91 chapters plus a detailed analysis of the supposed discrepancies, cross-referenced historical accounts, and detailed charts for ease of use. As with any history book, there are typographical errors in the text, but with three consecutive timelines running though the histories, it is very easy to arrive at the exact dates of recorded events. It is not surprising that this ancient document confirms the Scripture and the chronology given in the Hebrew version of the Old Testament, once and for all settling the chronology differences between the Hebrew Old Testament and the Greek Septuagint.

Third Corinthians
Ancient Gnostics and the End of the World

This little known, 2000-year-old Greek manuscript was used in the first two centuries to combat Gnostic cults. Whether or not it is an authentic copy of the original epistle written by the apostle Paul, it gives an incredible look into the cults that will arise in the Last Days. It contains a prophecy that the same heresies that pervaded the first century church would return before the Second Coming of the Messiah.

Ancient Paganism
The Sorcery of the Fallen Angels

Ancient Paganism explores the false religion of the ancient pre-Flood world and its spread into the Gentile nations after Noah's Flood. Quotes from the ancient church fathers, rabbis, and the Talmud detail the activities and beliefs of both Canaanite and New Testament era sorcery. This book explores how, according to biblical prophecy, this same sorcery will return before the Second Coming of Jesus Christ to earth. These religious beliefs and practices will invade the end time church and become the basis for the religion of the Antichrist. Wicca, Druidism, Halloween, Yule, meditation, and occultic tools are discussed at length.

The Rapture
The Pretribulational Rapture of the Church Viewed From the Bible and the Ancient Church

This book presents the doctrine of the pretribulational Rapture of the church. Many prophecies are explored with Biblical passages and terms explained.

Ancient Book of Daniel

Evidence is presented that proves the first century church believed the End Times would begin with the return of Israel to her ancient homeland, followed by the Tribulation and the Second Coming. More than fifty prophecies have been fulfilled since Israel became a nation.

Evidence is also given that several ancient rabbis and at least four ancient church fathers taught a pretribulational Rapture. This book also gives many of the answers to the arguments midtribulationists and posttribulationists use. It is our hope this book will be an indispensable guide for debating the doctrine of the Rapture.

Ancient Epistle of Barnabas
His Life and Teaching

The Epistle of Barnabas is often quoted by the ancient church fathers. Although not considered inspired Scripture, it was used to combat legalism in the first two centuries AD. Besides explaining why the Laws of Moses are not binding on Christians, the Epistle explains how many of the Old Testament rituals teach typological prophecy. Subjects explored are: Yom Kippur, the red heifer ritual, animal sacrifices, circumcision, the Sabbath, Daniel's visions and the end-time ten nation empire, and the temple.

The underlying theme is the Three-Fold Witness. Barnabas teaches that mature Christians must be able to lead people to the Lord, testify to others about Bible prophecy fulfilled in their lifetimes, and teach creation history and creation science to guard the faith against the false doctrine of evolution. This is one more ancient church document that proves the first century church was premillennial and constantly looking for the Rapture and other prophecies to be fulfilled.

The Ancient Church Fathers
What the Disciples of the Apostles Taught

This book reveals who the disciples of the twelve apostles were and what they taught, from their own writings. It documents the same doctrine was faithfully transmitted to their descendants in the first few centuries and where, when, and by whom, the doctrines began to change. The ancient church fathers make it very easy to know for sure what the complete teachings of Jesus and the twelve apostles were.

You will learn, from their own writings, what the first century disciples taught about the various doctrines that divide our church today. You will learn what was discussed at the seven general councils and why. You will learn about the cults and cult leaders who began to change doctrine and spread their heresy and how their teaching came to be the standard teaching in the medieval church. A partial list of doctrines discussed in this book are:

Abortion	Free will	Purgatory
Animals sacrifices	Gnostic cults	Psychology
Antichrist	Homosexuality	Reincarnation
Arminianism	Idolatry	Replacement theology
Bible or tradition	Islam	Roman Catholicism
Calvinism	Israel's return	The Sabbath
Circumcision	Jewish food laws	Salvation
Deity of Jesus Christ	Mary's virginity	Schism of Nepos
Demons	Mary's assumption	Sin / Salvation
Euthanasia	Meditation	The soul
Evolution	The Nicolaitans	Spiritual gifts
False gospels	Paganism	Transubstantiation
False prophets	Predestination	Yoga
Foreknowledge	Premillennialism	Women in ministry

For more information visit us at:

Biblefacts.org

Bibliography

Clearance Larkin, *Dispensational Truth*, 1907

Ken Johnson, *Ancient Prophecies Revealed*, Createspace, 2008

Ken Johnson, *The Rapture*, Createspace, 2009

Ken Johnson, *Ancient Paganism*, Createspace, 2009

Whiston, William, *The Works of Flavius Josephus*, London, Miller &
Sowerby, 1987. Includes Antiquies of the Jews.

Ken Johnson, *Ancient Seder Olam*, Createspace, 2006

Eerdmans Publishing, *Ante-Nicene Fathers*, Eerdmans Publishing,
1886

Cruse, C. F, *Eusebius' Ecclesiastical History*, Hendrickson
Publishers, 1998

CPSIA information can be obtained at www.ICGtesting.com
Printed in the USA
LVOW10s2241271213

367155LV00006B/26/P